Grilled
CHEESE

Grilled CHEESE

50 Recipes to Make You Melt

by **MARLENA SPIELER**

photographs by **SHERI GIBLIN**

CHRONICLE BOOKS

SAN FRANCISCO

Library of Congress
Cataloging-in-Publication
Data available.

ISBN 0-8118-4129-4

Manufactured in China.

Designed by Empire Design Studio
Prop styling by Leigh Noe
Food styling by Dan Becker
Photo assistant: Selena Aument
Typesetting by Empire Design Studio

Distributed in Canada by
Raincoast Books
9050 Shaughnessy Street
Vancouver, British Columbia V6P 6E5

10 9 8 7 6 5 4

Chronicle Books LLC
85 Second Street
San Francisco, California 94105

www.chroniclebooks.com

Acknowledgments

For Alan, for smiling hungrily when he sees me get the cheese and bread
ready; to Leah and Jon, for all the cheese cookin' in their NYC digs; to
Gretchen, for grilled cheese in San Francisco; to Nancy Fletcher of the
California Milk Advisory Board; to Patricia Schneider and Lynn
Devereaux, who shared good cheese and good times in California (it was
Patricia's idea for this book!). To Clark Wolf, for cheese thoughts and
inspirations, as well as those NYC margaritas. To Kathleen Iudice and Sue
Tonkin, for Paris panini, and to Berkeley's Cheeseboard—no mention
of the cheese in my life is complete without them. To Randall Hodgson, of
London's Neal's Yard Dairy, and a British cheese pioneer. To Auntie Stellie,
for those grilled Cheddar and dill pickle sandwiches; and to my mother,
for the grilled cheese and tomato soup lunches of childhood. To Juliet H.'s
love child, Angus.

Here's to cheesemaking's national treasure, Sonoma's Ig Vella; and to
Andante, Bellwether, Point Reyes Blue, Laura Chenel, Cowgirl Creamery,
Humboldt Fog, and all of the inspiring new waves of cheesemakers. To
Jenni Muir, for commissioning an Italian cheese article, to Anne Dettmer
for her Swiss cheese extravaganzas, and to Kim Severson for the cheese and
bread slumber party. To Ally Waks, Sandy Waks, Kamala Friedman, Esther
and John, Paula Aspin and her Chris, Sheona and Tony Vianello, Portia
Smith, Antonietta Kelly, and Emi Kazuko and the Sam's Deli gang: Etty,
Bruce, and Natalie Blackman, famous for their grilled cheese. To Amy
Treadwell and Holly Burrows and the publishing crew at Chronicle Books
for all the hard work. Most specially, here's to Michael Bauer, Miriam
Morgan, and the rest of the *San Francisco Chronicle* food department—
the most wonderful colleagues anyone could hope for.

And a huge melted cheese–smeared thanks to Bill LeBlond, who thought
that this lighthearted, cheese-filled book just might be a lot of fun to pub-
lish, and even more fun to eat through.

Contents

Austin Powers' Shag-a-delic: 1970s Grilled Ham, Cheese, and Pineapple, PAGE 59

Crisply toasted in the pan or broiled open-face to a melty sizzle, there are few things more enticing than a grilled cheese sandwich.

The golden brown toast crunches on the outside as you bite into it, yielding its soft, hot, oozing cheese. You get a rush of pleasure and a shiver of both the forbidden and the familiar: that buttery crispness of earthy bread with its layer of melting warm cheese. Cheese and buttered toast may well be a dietary luxury these days, perhaps even taboo for some; yet grilled cheese sandwiches are the culinary equivalent of a comfort blanket. A grilled cheese sandwich is probably what your mother fed you, your school fed you, and your childhood fed you. And it just might be what you feed yourself and close friends and family, at least occasionally.

Grilled cheese sandwiches can be one of the simplest things to make, something you can make at almost any hour with ingredients right there in your kitchen already, in less than a few minutes. Breakfast, lunch, dinner, after school, or midnight snack . . . all are the perfect time for a grilled cheese sandwich.

The whole world—at least wherever they have both bread and cheese—loves a grilled cheese sandwich.

In France, grilled cheese may be the rustic *casse croûtes* (midmorning snacks) eaten outdoors by workers in the field, or the chic little grilled truffle and *fromage* that *toute* Paris has been nibbling recently. Too, grilled cheese sandwiches are one of France's national café treats: *croque monsieur*. Ranging from simple ham-filled thin white bread topped with cheese and melted, to an extravaganza of excellent cheese, perhaps moistened with a bit of cream, a smudge of bechamel sauce, all melted atop *pain au levain* (such as the superb sourdough loaf of Pôilane). Croque monsieur is an entire family of grilled cheese sandwich possibilities. Additions such as country ham (*croque compagnard*), ratatouille or a slice of tomato (*croque Provençal*), Spanish chorizo (*croque señor*), or Cantal cheese and country ham (*croque Auvergnate*) all transform this simple sandwich, as does the classic *croque madame*, in which the sandwich is topped with a fried egg.

Then there are Italian panini taking the world by storm. A soft roll filled with cheese and a wide variety of meats, spreads, and condiments, pressed between the heavy hot metal plates of the panini press, yields crisp golden bread, filled with gloriously melted cheese.

Across the sea to Florida, Cuban sandwiches are all the rage: hot, flat, oozing cheese, full of cured meats, pickles, and tons of flavor—clearly a cousin to the *bocadillo* I ate in a café in Ibiza, Spain.

Welsh Rarebit is England's classic grilled cheese offering: melting, spiced Cheddar on toast. In Umbria melted fontina is cossetted with cream and truffles, and then spooned over bruschetta—divine (especially with artichokes). And in a northern Italian vineyard, I joined grape pickers making a late-morning snack of shredded fontina, fresh rosemary, and diced pancetta, smeared atop a doughy flatbread and toasted over an open fire.

And if you happen to come upon a casse croûte of Roquefort in France's southwest, don't miss the chance: Roquefort, Gruyère, and a splash of wine melted onto a toasty baguette—or simply open these pages and make one yourself.

Mexico and Southwest America's quesadilla, the Indian's love affair with pizza (tandoori pizza!), the labna-filled mannakish of Lebanon, and Turkey's cheese-stuffed flatbreads are all versions of the grilled cheese sandwich. Sometimes I think the whole world of bread and cheese needs only to be paired up and melted for another wonderful foray into grilled cheese bliss. The application of heat—and sometimes, a brainstorm of creativity—transforms the two most basic foodstuffs, bread and cheese, into a toasty, gooey, and crisp culinary experience.

American Grilled Cheese—
Childhood and Rediscovery

As hip and varied as grilled cheese sandwiches may be today, when we were growing up, a grilled cheese sandwich was what you had as a rainy-day lunch with tomato soup (unless you were very lucky and your mother decided to make soup and sandwich for supper instead of the usual meat and potatoes). I remember tuna melt with a feeling akin to jubilation—melted cheese with soft creamy tuna salad, snuggled into crisp buttered toasted bread, felt like a celebration instead of a meal.

I know I'm not alone in this. For, after eating our way through the world's street food and ethnic specialties, from sushi and dim sum to tacos and burritos, doro wat, momos, pho, stir-fried tofu, falafel, and pasta fagioli, sitting down to a good ol' grilled cheese sandwich is like coming home. Just the thought of it makes me want to run into the kitchen right now, and grill up a taste of familiarity—with a big dose of modern flavors and attitude.

The traditional format of bread + cheese + a hot pan (or hot broiler), with our contemporary variety of cheeses and breads, and savory additions creates dazzling grilled cheese sandwiches.

Where to Find Them

Coast to coast, the coolest American cafés and bistros present grilled cheese sandwiches, not just as an after-thought, but also as signature dishes.

New York's Craftbar serves a wild mushroom, duck prosciutto, and melted Taleggio cheese; in New York, too, Tabla's Bread Bar serves grilled tandoori Cheddar; Campanile in L.A. has grilled cheese night and Michael Mina offers lobster grilled cheese at his restaurant Arcadia, in San Jose; in Sonoma, California, The Girl and the Fig offers a grilled cheese sandwich on their "lunch menu of the day," and San Francisco's Tartine serves a croque monsieur with béchamel as you seldom find it in Paris these days. But no restaurant matches the devotion to this homey little dish better than Grilled Cheese NYC (Ludlow, near Houston Street), a lunch café devoted almost entirely to the grilled cheese sandwich. At lunchtime the little room is filled with the happy buzz of grilled cheese sandwich munching.

Grilled cheese sandwiches make chic and enticing cocktail party fare—think small, and crisp, and oozing indulgence. Think Venice's legendary Harry's Bar, where elegant little fingers of thinly sliced, crustless grilled cheese sandwiches are served with great aplomb.

Whether homey and familiar or delicate and posh, a grilled cheese sandwich is simply one of the most enticing morsels on earth.

SAGE SAUSAGE AND JACK CHEESE, PAGE 74

Making Grilled Cheese Sandwiches

You don't really need special gizmos, though there are some nifty ones that create a crisp outside with melty cheese within. There are presses that squish fat rolls, excellent for Italian panini, Cuban sandwiches, bocadillos, and plain old grilled cheese. And there are sandwich makers that press the outside edges of bread tightly, tightly, oh so tightly together to enclose molten hot melted cheese. (The latter were very popular in Great Britain in the sixties—I am told there wasn't a household without one.) But truly, a good heavy skillet—preferably nonstick—does the trick for pan-browned grilled cheese sandwiches and a broiler works perfectly for open-faced ones.

Though grilled cheese sandwiches can be no more than pan-browned bread and cheese, a little embellishment takes them onto a completely different plane: stimulating, exciting, dare I say, thrilling?

Few can resist such crisp, golden, oozing temptation; I know I never can.

A Guide to the GRILLED

The Cheese: Which type to choose?

The main criterion for choosing your cheese is whether or not it melts.

Not all cheeses do melt. Hispanic cheeses such as *panela* don't melt; neither do Cypriot *anari*, *halloumi*, or an Italian mountain cheese such as the one I once ate in Assisi roasted over an open fire. Such cheeses are delicious served sizzling on their own, but are useless in grilled cheese sandwiches.

On the other hand, very creamy cheeses, delicate in flavor, soft and velvety in texture, are nearly melting already. They don't keep their character and integrity inside a grilled cheese sandwich. Pair them with another firmer, more assertive, sassier cheese.

Most firm sliceable cheeses are game for the grilling and can be used interchangeably with others of similar character.

To help choose, here is a mini-guide of cheese types, categorized by flavor and texture.

Note: While I've placed certain cheeses in certain groups, many of the cheeses can be placed into several categories at the same time.

FRESH CHEESES do not undergo a ripening process. These include cottage cheese, cream cheese, mascarpone, soft goat cheese, *fromage blanc*, Quark, Indian *panir*, *Robiola*, Spanish and Hispanic *Requeson*, ricotta, or the simple yogurt cheese, labna.

Fresh cheeses are mild, milky, and soft; if used in grilled cheese sandwiches they tend to run uncontrollably, so need to be paired with a firmer, more robust cheese.

There is also a family of fresh cheeses that are made from pressed curds and therefore do not melt: Indian *panir* is such a cheese, as is the Cypriot *anari*, and Hispanic *panela*. Freshly made pecorino is similar.

Fresh mozzarella, on the other hand, was made for melting into seductive chewy strings, pizza-style. (And while we all know how delicious it is with tomatoes, garlic, and Italian flavors, try making mozzarella cheese sandwiches with Mexican salsa, or with Indian "curry" spicing).

Feta cheese, from Greece, Israel, or Bulgaria, along with Turkish *beyas peynir*, Romanian *brynza*, and Spanish *queso de Bourgos*, is a semi-fresh cheese made from pressed curds; it melts partially, and is delicious in grilled cheese sandwiches when paired with other more meltable cheeses such as Jack or mozzarella. Always buy sheep's milk feta, or a combination of sheep and goat feta, for its rich texture and excellent balance of sharp and mild. *Manouri* is another fresh sheep's milk cheese from Greece; if you find it, have a taste—once hooked, you'll find endless opportunities for enjoying it.

Double and triple crème cheeses are heavily enriched with cream—double crèmes have 60% butterfat content, while triple crèmes have 75%. Lusciously rich, they can be either unaged or ripened to a nicely assertive character such as *Boursault*, *St. Andre*, *Brillat-Savarin*, and *Explorateur*.

For grilled cheese sandwiches, these are best simply layered onto hot toast and allowed to gently melt from the heat of the toast, rather than cooked in a pan.

Bland, mild, and easily melted cheeses are mild in flavor, softly supple, and semi-firm in texture. The list includes Dutch Edam and Gouda, Hispanic *mennonita* and *Asadero*, *Bel Paese*, Muenster, and domestic or Danish fontina (the Italian original has more assertive flavor). And when it comes to Monterey Jack, Ig Vella's Jack is always, deservedly, a prize winner, as is the Sierra Nevada Cheese Company's.

Provolone, *provatura*, and *scamorza* are all mild Italian cheeses, often made into the classic Roman grilled cheese treat: layered onto bread, topped with an anchovy or two, then broiled until sizzling.

Softish, ripened flavorful cheeses include *Reblochon*, *Tommes*, *Chaumes*, and *Tomme de Montagne*, as well as the monastery cheeses. Developed over centuries in Europe's monasteries, they include *Port Salut*, *Saint Paulin*, *Esrom*, *Tilsit*, and Havarti. They are rich and delicate; some, such as *Taleggio* and the whole *Stracchino* family, veer into the quite rich and ever-so-stinky—though delicious—category.

SWISS-STYLE CHEESES usually have tough hard rinds and interiors dotted with holes caused by the expansion of gas within the cheese curd during the ripening period. *Emmentaler*, probably the most famous, has a tough outer rind, distinctive holes or "eyes," and characteristic mild, sweetish, nutty flavor. *Appenzell*, Gruyère, *Sbrinz*, *Beaufort*, *Comté*, and *raclette* are all kissin' cousins. Do yourself a favor and buy well-made, artisanal Swiss-style cheeses (usually imported from Switzerland and France's Jura). You will be rewarded in nutty, grassy flavors that burst upon your palate; you will likely wonder what you saw in plain "ol' Swiss cheese" in the first place. Other made for grilling cheeses include Norwegian Jarlsberg and the Greek graviera.

FIRM, FULL-FLAVORED CHEESES are golden and flavorful, yet not stinking; these cheeses melt deliciously. They may be cow's, goat's, or sheep's milk, or a combination of all three. Spanish manchego, medium *Asiago*, *Mahon*, aged Gouda, *Idiazabal*, *Ossau Iraty Brebis*, Italian fontina, *caciocavallo*, *Montasio*, *tomme de Savoie*, and Ig Vella's delectable *mezzo secco*, or a partially aged Sonoma Jack—all are worth seeking out.

CHEDDAR-STYLE CHEESES are some of the most widely made cheeses in the world. The term Cheddar refers to the process of cheese making in which infant cheeses have been cut into pieces, stacked, and turned at the bottom of the cheese vat. Then the aging is continued. A good example of the cheese will be firm in texture, with a clear, mellow taste.

When young, Cheddar is mild, softish, and somewhat rubbery; as it matures it develops a sharp and tangy bite as well as an element of dryish crumbliness. In America much Cheddar is orange (colored with *annato*, a harmless spice used for tinting cheese as well as margarine and butter). Colby is a marbled cream- and orange-colored Cheddar. On the other hand, in Canada, England, Scotland, Wales, Australia, New Zealand, etc., Cheddar is creamy yellow-white.

America makes delicious Cheddars, from the west coast to the Midwest and the Pacific Northwest. Crowley Cheese company in Vermont is America's oldest. They've been making Cheddar for the past 120 years. Meanwhile, the huge—14 million pounds a year—cheese-making Cabot has been going strong since 1919. In addition, small artisanal cheese makers are popping up coast to coast.

English cheeses such as Gloucester, Cheshire, Leicester, Lancashire, Derby, Wensleydale, and Caerphilly all belong to the Cheddar family. Wensleydale and Caerphilly, however, are tangier and crumblier, less meltable (pair them with a creamier cheese for grilled cheese sandwiches).

Raw milk Cheddars are divine (Britain's Montgomery's Cheddar is exquisite); *Cantal* and *Mimolette* are two French Cheddar cheeses very different in flavor and color (Cantal pale yellow, Mimolette bright orange). The Greek *kashkaval* is made from the Cheddaring technique, using sheep's milk.

EXTRA-HARD CHEESES, such as Parmesan, aged Asiago, *locatelli Romano,* pecorino (made from sheep's milk), mountain cheeses from the Greek islands such as kofalotiri, *grana,* dry Jack, Sbrinz, *Cotija,* and *Enchilado* are all known for their exceptionally hard texture and their strong, sharp flavor. Some—such as Parmesan—have a slightly nutty flavor. Younger versions of some of these cheeses can be eaten fresh as table cheeses.

Most of these cheeses need to be finely grated or shaved for optimum meltability.

BLUE-VEINED CHEESES are characterized by a flesh veined with blue, blue-green, or green, as well as pungent aromas and tangy flavors. All blue-veined cheeses are internally ripened after being inoculated with a *Penicillium* spore. They can vary from soft to crumbly in texture. Roquefort, *Fourme d'Ambert, bleu des Causse,* Stilton, Gorgonzola, *Cabrales,* Blue Castello, Point Reyes, and Maytag are delicious, personality-filled blues. Danish Blue is a great workhorse of a blue: strong in flavor, and what it lacks in delicacy isn't missed once the cheese is layered and melted into a grilled cheese sandwich. Scotland produces some wonderful blues (treat yourself to a heavenly nibble of a true Lanarkshire Blue), as do Ireland (Cashell) and England (besides the rich Stilton, Oxford blue is "delish"); and if you have a chance to sample it, Shropshire is a delicious blue-veined English Cheddar.

BLOOMY OR FLOWERY-RIND CHEESES such as Camembert, Brie, *Coulommiers,* and *Affinois/pavé d'Affinois* are thus named because of the light, downy white rind that grows on their surfaces, the result of their being treated with the *Penicillium* candidate spore. The inside of these cheeses should be soft and the color of hay, or rich cream. As it ages, the inside of the cheese—called the paste—grows runny and can ooze when cut, especially at warm room temperature.

Small individual flowery-rind cheeses have great character, such as the magnificent *St. Marcellin* cheese. With its affinity for truffles, it is delicious spread onto a truffle-anointed croûte.

GOAT AND SHEEP CHEESES are distinctly different in taste from cow's milk cheeses. In general they have a whiff of the barnyard (a "goaty" or "sheepish" quality to their flavor). They may be fresh and tangy, or formed and aged to a variety of shapes and sizes. Goat and sheep cheeses are both made into pyramids, rounds, cones, and discs, while goat cheese is often sold in long cylinders. Sometimes sheep and goat cheeses are wrapped in vine or other fragrant leaves, such as the chestnut-leaf-wrapped *banon*, or coated in herbs, such as the rosemary-coated sheep's milk *Brin d'Amour*.

Sheep cheeses are sometimes formed into large wheels on their own or mixed with other milks. Idiazábal from the Basque country and Spain's manchego are delicious examples.

France (*chèvre*), America (especially California), the UK (especially Wales), and Spain (*queso de cabra*) produce excellent goat's cheeses, while sheep cheeses are represented fabulously by Basque Ossau Iraty Brebis, Greek/Balkan/Israeli kashkaval, and Greek *kasseri* (all delicious in grilled cheese sandwiches).

Goat's and sheep's milk, or a combination including cow's milk, may be made as Brie-type cheese, too. Individual matured goat's and sheep's milk discs such as *Felicien*, *picodon*, or crottins are delicious sizzled under the broiler, then served hot and melting on top of a crunchy croûte, plopped into a crisp leafy salad.

And a slightly aged, yet still creamy and soft, goat cheese paired with walnuts, then pressed into a panini, is one of the most enticing treats you could find on the streets of Paris today.

SPICED OR FLAVORED CHEESES are eschewed by many, but I refuse to be such a snob. In fact, cheeses that may be brash and vulgar on a cheese board are perfection melted in between the covers of bread. Derby Sage with its green scent of sage, Leyden shot through with cumin seeds, onion-and-chive-spiked Double Gloucester, dill-speckled Havarti, as well as the flavored Jacks (garlic, hot pepper, and pesto), are all delish as grilled cheese.

SMOKED CHEESES can be any kind of cheese, treated with wood smoke. I find them too harsh, especially when the smoke flavor is produced by chemicals applied to the cheese, though if smoked naturally over a fire they can be fine. Provolone and mozzarella both take nicely to smoking (and are especially good in a sandwich with caramelized onions in a bit of balsamic vinegar).

STRONG-SMELLING CHEESES, such as Limburger, stinking Bishop, *Maroilles*, *Livarot*, *Pont l'Eveque*, and *Epoisses*, might not be sociable additions to every grilled cheese sandwich, but slapped in between thin slices of black pumpernickel with paper-thin slices of onion, or layered onto toasted baguette . . . mmmmmm.

PROCESSED CHEESE is usually made from one or two different cheese types blended together, then whirled and heated. As a result, its ripening process is arrested. It can never develop individual character, because the microorganisms that create such things are lost in the processing.

American cheese is probably the most famous processed cheese. Don't expect to find it in this book. Why choose processed cheese when there are so many fabulous cheeses to choose from?

Buying, Sourcing, and Storing

Take yourself to the best cheese shop you can find (or to the cheese counter in the supermarket), and return regularly to taste, taste, taste, and taste some more. Most cheese shops will encourage your cheese sampling and discoveries; it's the best cheese education you'll ever find.

Farmer's markets that sell artisanal cheeses might invite you to the farm, too. Keep your cheese sourcing as personal as possible, as the mutual interest between cheese maker/seller and cheese-eater will enhance your education and enjoyment.

Once purchased, cheese should be stored in the refrigerator. Cheese should also be protected from moisture loss. Plastic film is good only for the short term, as it does not let the cheese breathe. If left too long, bacteria build up on the cheese's surface. If cutting a whole large cheese, cover only the cut area with plastic wrap.

For blue cheese, use foil for wrapping. Blues can get unappealingly sweaty in plastic.

Special cheese containers are good; though take care when storing different cheeses together. Never store blue cheese or any other strong cheese with other milder ones. Cheese should be enjoyed at room temperature. Common sense tells you that cold cheese melts more slowly than does room-temperature cheese.

Next: Choose a Bread

Choose a bread that matches the qualities of your cheese in thickness as well as flavor. Cheeses that melt easily and run willingly need to have thinly sliced bread—thick bread requires too long in the pan; your delicate cheese will run out, leaving stodgy cheese-smeared bread. With thin slices, it's into the pan, brown and crisp quickly, then onto your plate! Thick slices of bread are best for thick slices of sharp cheese.

Following is a mini-guide to start you off.

SOURDOUGH BREAD, *pain au levain,* baguette, *pugliese,* and soft rolls (both sour and sweet) are best with most cheese and strongly flavored additions. Try Mahon, Roquefort or other robust blues, goat cheeses, Gruyère and other Swiss-type cheeses, caciocavallo, and any of the sharp Cheddar cheeses. Sourdough and baguette are delectable with Gouda or Jack and zesty condiments, such as olive paste, mustards, relishes, salsas, and chutneys.

PITA, MIDDLE EASTERN FLATBREADS, *piadina,* and tortillas are at their best with strong flavors—tomato, pesto, and salsa—and all sorts of cheeses like Jack, fontina, mozzarella, goat cheeses, the blues family, manchego, mezzo secco, caciocavallo, and Idiazábal. A combination of two cheeses in these breads is especially good. Try feta and Jack, Humboldt Fog and fontina, or ricotta and manchego.

Wholesome whole-grain breads such as oatmeal, whole wheat, multigrain, and sprouted wheatberry make wonderful partners for the Cheddar family, as well as the mildish, semi-firm cheeses such as Jack, Gouda, manchego, Idiazábal, Havarti, and medium Asiago. Or flavored cheeses such as garlic Jack or dill Havarti.

Hearty, earthy breads such as rye and pumpernickel, whole-wheat and rye pain au levain, and walnut breads are good with the Swiss family of cheeses. Sharp Cheddar, manchego, Mahon, Idiazábal, and pungent blues are great choices. Briny feta with a bit of cream cheese and shredded Jack melted onto hearty rye ìs invigorating.

FLAVORED BREADS are great in grilled cheese sandwiches. Greek sesame-onion bread, rosemary, dill-weed bread, olive bread, sun-dried tomato *batard,* multi-seeded baguette, onion bread, and hazelnut bread—all propose grilled cheese possibilities. Try garlic Jack on sun-dried tomato bread, with a few leaves of basil tucked in; Taleggio on hazelnut bread, with a slice or two of prosciutto; manchego or fontina on seeded baguette; manouri on Greek seeded bread; caciocavallo, provolone, and mozzarella on rosemary bread.

FRUITY BREADS such as raisin bread, *pannetone,* fruitcake, and fig and fennel-seed sourdough are delicious with tangy goat cheese, mild melty Jack, bland Bel Paese and Port-Salut, lightly sweetened ricotta, medium Asiago, and manchego. Cheddar is particularly good on raisin bread.

BAGELS AND ENGLISH MUFFINS are both terrific open-faced, toasted and melted with rich cheese. English muffins are good for tuna melts or that '60s classic, English muffin pizza. And bagels . . . try a garlic bagel topped with Brie, Camembert, or Coulommiers, a pumpernickel bagel topped with goat cheese, or an onion bagel with feta and fresh herbs. Never make a closed grilled cheese sandwich using an English muffin or a bagel. The melted cheese will squeeze out and you will end up chewing the heaviest food on earth.

FOCACCIA and *ciabatta* are both flattish Italian breads, both endlessly delicious in grilled cheese sandwiches. Focaccia is much like a thick pizza, while ciabatta is like an airy batard, with large air holes and very tender insides. Focaccia is often flavored with green onions, tomatoes, herbs, or cheeses. Ciabatta might be studded with olives, sun-dried tomatoes, or walnuts.

GOOD-QUALITY PLAIN SLICED WHITE BREAD with a firm close-textured crumb is the best thing most grilled cheese sandwiches could want. Use a cheese that is spunky enough to enliven the sandwich—sharp Cheddar and all of its permutations comes to mind, as does Jarlsberg and the milder Swiss family. Add a zesty embellishment: sliced onion, tomato, watercress, chutneys, and/or interesting, lively mustards.

Auntie Stelli's Open-Faced Grilled Cheddar and Dill Pickle, **PAGE 38**

That Little Extra Something

Think of your grilled cheese sandwich as a little black dress. Or for guys, a pair of jeans. Dress it up, or dress it down; it is as at home for a genteel tea party as it is for a swank Saturday-night bash, or a funky morning-after brunch. Accessories—i.e. the condiments, relishes, etc.—are all important, but the little black dress (read bread and cheese) is the basis of it all.

In grilled cheese sandwich terms, this means everything you add to hot bread and cheese transforms it. It also gives you an excuse to indulge yourself in the latest, most alluring goodies that call to you from the grocer's shelf, begging to be tucked into your shopping bag.

Following is a guide of suggestions and combinations.

VINEGARY PICKLES, such as dilled cucumbers, *giardiniera* (Italian or Mexican mixed vegetables with jalapeño), roasted peppers, piccalilli, and pickled onions, all help enliven mild-flavored cheeses such as Jack, Edam, and Gouda, and help balance the sharpness of a nice strong Cheddar, Cheshire, or Wensleydale.

OLIVES, SUN-DRIED TOMATOES, pickled garlic, artichoke hearts, olive spreads such as tapenade, Greek pickled peppers, and pesto all enhance bland Mediterranean cheeses: mozzarella, scamorza, provolone, and Jack.

SWEET, TANGY, SPICY PICKLES such as bread-and-butter pickles, little red "Pepp-a-dew" peppers, or Bransten's Pickle enhance the sharpness of a nice strong Cheddar, as well as Gouda and Edam.

MUSTARD: Nothing dresses a grilled cheese sandwich as perfectly as a well-chosen, interesting mustard. Either spread inside the sandwich or serve on the side to dab at. Try sweet Russian mustard with Jarlsberg cheese; green tarragon, or herbes de Provence, or red pepper Provençal mustard with any mild slicing cheese like Jack, Gouda, fontina, or Havarti. Creole, being quite a zippy little mustard, is delicious with any funky sliceable cheese. But, remember that a wimpy cheese will be overshadowed.

SWEET-TANGY HOMEMADE CHUTNEYS, made with simmered onions and dried fruit, oomphed with vinegar, sugar, and spices, make a perfect accompaniment to grilled cheese sandwiches, either spread inside or on the side for dabbing. Onions and dried cherries are delicious with blue or goat cheese. Pineapple chutney is terrific with Cheddar, as is Major Grey's, while beet marmalade is sublime with toasted Roquefort sandwiches.

VEGETABLES—raw, roasted, sautéed, or grilled—are fabulous in grilled cheese sandwiches. Sautéed mushrooms or diced truffles are divine with young goat cheese, or a well-aged Comté. Garlicky spinach is great with dill Havarti, mozzarella, or Jack; a slice of tomato, a handful of watercress leaves or arugula, and a leaf or two of red or white endive are good with almost any cheese. And why stop there? Raw onions? Chopped garlic? Yes, yes, yes!

A SLICE OR TWO OF CURED MEATS, poultry, and fish can transform even the simplest grilled cheese sandwich. Try *jamon serrano* added to manchego or Idiazábal; pastrami to Jarlsberg; Italian salami or Spanish *chorizo* to Jack or fontina; grilled *merguez* to fontina; smoked turkey to Stilton; a salty fillet of anchovy to provatura or provolone.

SALSA: Spunky salsas—red, green, or smoky chipotle—spike up mild melting cheeses on baguettes and rolls.

FRESH FRUIT, such as very thinly sliced apples, pears, figs, and other firm fruit, add a sweet tangy freshness to any strongly flavored cheese, especially the blues family.

Putting It Together

The Cheese: When to Slice, When to Shred?

SLICED CHEESE keeps its character as it melts in the sandwich. This is the best way to make sandwiches if you are making a simple combination of bread and cheese with or without the addition of condiments, vegetables, and/or cured meats.

SHREDDING is good for hard cheeses that otherwise wouldn't melt, or for when you want a combination of hard cheeses mixed together. A dab of sour cream, onions, spices, or aromatic herbs combines with the cheese for oozing flavor in each bite.

Cutting Sandwiches

While a grilled cheese sandwich is fetching served whole, on a plate, cut into triangle-shaped halves or quarters, it is even more appealing. Cut it into festive shapes, and be charmed!

For all cutting, use a very sharp knife to slice through the sandwich quickly, crisply, and neatly. A knife that is even the tiniest bit dull can tear apart your beautiful sandwich.

For delicate sandwiches, the sort you'd enjoy with a glass of red wine for a sociable get-together, use thinly sliced bread (it gets crispier) with the crusts cut off. *Voilà*: crisp little canapés.

ELEGANT LITTLE FINGER SANDWICHES Cut crustless bread into strips about 2 inches in width; you should get about three fingers per slice of bread. Assemble into sandwiches, then pan brown in a hot skillet, pressing down on them with a spatula as they brown.

TRIANGLES Remove the crust from the bread, make into sandwiches, then cut diagonally into halves or quarters before browning.

ROUNDS Cut the layered bread and cheese into rounds using a cookie cutter. Assemble into sandwiches and pan brown.

STARS Use a cookie cutter or sharp knife to cut the bread and cheese, then assemble and brown, for very charming, star-shaped grilled cheese sandwiches. (Brown the extra tidbits and you'll have a tasty treat for the cook.)

If making these grilled cheese goodies in large amounts for a party, brush the outsides with olive oil or melted butter, then place in a 350-375ºF oven to bake rather than browning them individually in a hot pan.

CRISP OPEN-FACED CANAPÉS Top thinly sliced sourdough baguette, cocktail rye bread, or any bread cut into fingers with a grated cheese mixture, then broil until bubbling and melted, the bread crisp at its edges.

Basic How-To: Flash in the Pan

Brush the outsides of the sandwiches with olive oil or spread very lightly with softened butter. Place them into a heavy nonstick skillet over medium heat (adjust the heat according to how fast the sandwiches are browning and melting).

Important Tip: Weighting the sandwiches presses the bread with the cheese and other fillings, resulting in a crisper, more compact, sandwich. You can press the sandwiches either by weighting them with something heavy—such as a skillet or wide-bottomed saucepan—or a flat lid just the right size to fit snugly on top of the sandwiches, with a weight laid on top. A couple of cans of food work well as weights, as does a tea kettle filled with water, or simply applying a small amount of pressure by pushing on top of the covering pan. Alternatively, if no second pan or weight is available, simply press on each sandwich every so often using a flat spatula.

A built-in griddle should be treated as a skillet. Brown your sandwich and weight it as above.

Ridged grill pans, especially the ones lined in a nonstick coating, give a nice grill mark to the sandwich. They are best when the cheese is firmer and less likely to ooze and run out of the sandwich uncontrollably as it melts. Clean the pan between sandwiches to rid it of bits of melted cheese; otherwise, they will turn into morsels of charcoal as you brown the next sandwich.

Sandwiches pan browned in a skillet or ridged grill pan need to be turned, once or twice, for even crisping and melting. Use a spatula, and if sandwiches seem likely to slide from the spatula, use your hand carefully to stabilize it on the spatula as you flip.

Sandwich Presses

Sandwich presses or panini presses come with their own directions. Basically, brush the sandwiches very lightly with oil or melted butter, place the sandwiches on the bottom of the press, then close the hot top of the press according to directions. They will emerge browned, crisp, oozing, and gooey.

Choosing a Sandwich Maker

If you should so decide to, here are a few suggestions:

SALTON SANDWICH MAKER Seals the edges of the sandwich and gives a good toasty finish.

GEORGE FOREMAN GRILLING MACHINE Not bad at all, and you might already have one lurking in your kitchen.

KRUPS PANINI GRILL Makes two sandwiches at a time, resulting in a crisp exterior with nice grill marks. It's on the expensive side, but if you really like pressed grilled cheese sandwiches, you might want to make the investment.

WAFFLE IRONS Leave a weird pattern of square indentations, which can tear slices of bread, though they're not bad for rolls. Waffle irons are a mess to clean if cheese oozes out, however. Some waffle irons have removable indentation grids that convert to a flat griddle for grilled sandwich making.

Confession: I have purchased a Hello Kitty Sandwich Maker. It was not cheap ($39.99), but makes the most adorable sandwiches—each one with a Hello Kitty imprinted on its crisp toast. Good only for little triangle-shaped sealed sandwiches, but so darned cute!

Tips for the Perfect Grilled Cheese Sandwich

1 Don't be tempted to melt lots of butter in the pan and fry the sandwiches. As good an idea as it might seem initially, the bread will absorb too much fat and your sandwich will be heavy, heavy, heavy. Instead, lightly brush a little olive oil (plain or extra-virgin) or melted butter onto the outside of both pieces of bread.

2 If using a panini press, you will only need a tiny bit of oil brushed on the surface initially, then none at all as long as the press is hot and the bread is not sticking.

3 Use a heavy nonstick skillet. I'm in love with my 12-inch Calphalon pan. It is perfect for grilled cheese sandwiches (and it's pretty wonderful for other cooking needs too).

4 Slow, even cooking: Go for a long, slow crisping rather than a fast fry. However, cooking the sandwich for too long can risk burning the bread, and nothing will save a burnt grilled sandwich.

5 Amounts of fillings: You need to use your eyes and good judgment here, as many breads are different sizes. Don't be a slave to the amounts of cheese listed in any recipe. Most sandwiches will take about 2 ounces of cheese.

6 For really crisp sandwiches, such as the tiny canapé types made with thinly sliced baguette, use stale bread; it absorbs less fat and crisps up better.

7 Place the cheese on top of the bread carefully for a relatively even fit; too much cheese hanging over the edge will melt and blob out. Though this is delicious melted into bubbly, crisp, cheesy bits in the pan, it's messy.

8 Open-faced sandwiches should be placed on a baking sheet under a preheated broiler; if there are several levels, place it on the highest. You may also place it on the top shelf of a hot (450-500ºF) oven. Though the idea of a microwave might be tempting, resist it. The cheese may melt moltenly, but it will never sizzle and get those delicious crispy brown bits. And the bread will never, ever toast, only grow chewy and tough.

9 When making sandwiches in a roll or baguette, remove some of the middle of the soft bread to accommodate the fillings.

10 Distribute the filling evenly and flatten the sandwich gently with your hands before you brush it with oil and brown it.

11 Make ahead: You can't make grilled cheese sandwiches ahead of time and reheat—they grow soggy. You can, however, assemble the sandwiches ahead of time and cook them at the last minute.

Spinach and Dill Havarti on Multigrain Bread or Focaccia, PAGE 37

Five-Minute Wonders

Grilled Cheese Sandwiches with Five Ingredients or Less

Take five ingredients—including the bread, cheese, and oil for brushing—sandwich them together, and sizzle them in a pan. A great example of how a simple little sandwich can be sensational; it's all about the excellence of interesting and yummy ingredients rather than any culinary acrobatics.

Taleggio and Fontina
with the Scent of
White Truffle

8 thinnish slices of Italian country-style white bread

3–4 tablespoons white truffle paste or other truffle or truffle-porcini condimento

4 ounces Taleggio cheese, sliced

4 ounces fontina cheese, sliced

Soft butter for spreading on bread

Truffle and cheese, melted into a little sandwich, is delicious cut into fingers and eaten as a morsel to go with the afternoon's *aperitivo*, or as lunch alongside Spring Mix with Herbs (page 103). Truffle paste, with or without wild mushroom *porcini*, is also known as *condimento*, a savory spread of truffles, olive oil, and other aromatics. Buy it at specialty shops or well-equipped grocery stores. Since garlic has such an affinity for white truffle, sometimes I toss a little chopped garlic into the truffle paste or simply into the pan when the sandwiches are freshly made.

1 Lightly spread 1 side of each slice of bread with truffle paste. Top 4 of the slices with the Taleggio and fontina, then top each with another truffle paste-spread bread.

2 Lightly spread butter on the outside of each sandwich, then heat a panini press or a heavy nonstick skillet over medium-high heat. Brown the sandwiches, turning once or twice, until the bread is crisp and golden and the cheese has melted.

3 Serve immediately, fragrant with truffle and oozing melted cheese, cut into quarters or dainty bars.

This is also good made on sourdough if rye bread is not your thing. Me? I could eat anything between the covers of two soft fragrant slices of rye . . . but then again, I feel that way about sourdough, too. And come to think of it, I feel that way about cheese.

If green olive tapenade is not on your shelf, purée about ¼ cup of pitted green olives (stuffed or unstuffed—it doesn't really matter) with a tablespoon or two of extra-virgin olive oil, until it forms a paste. If you can't be bothered whirling, just slice the olives and sprinkle instead of spread.

Moroccan Carrot Relish (page 103) makes a nice side accompaniment for this zippy sandwich.

2 tablespoons green olive tapenade

3 tablespoon mild Dijon mustard

8 slices seeded rye bread

8–10 ounces Jack cheese, or other mild white cheese (such as Havarti or Edam), sliced

Olive oil for brushing bread

1 Mix the tapenade with the mustard in a small bowl.

2 Lay out the bread and spread 4 of the slices on one side only with the tapenade mustard to taste. Top with the cheese and the second piece of bread, then press together well.

3 Lightly brush the outside of each sandwich with the olive oil, then brown in a sandwich maker, panini press, or heavy nonstick skillet, weighted down (see Tip, page 22) to press the sandwiches as they brown. Cook over medium-high heat until lightly crisped on the outside and the cheese is melting within.

4 Serve hot and sizzling, golden brown.

VARIATION *Grilled Jack on Whole Wheat with Giardiniera Relish*

Omit the green olive tapenade and substitute 2 to 3 tablespoons finely chopped pickled Italian vegetables (known as giardiniera; similar pickled vegetables are eaten in Mexico and although spicier, can be used in place of the giardiniera). Make the sandwiches on whole-grain bread, preferably one with whole sprouted grains.

Grilled Jack on Rye
with Green Olive Mustard

Radicchio, Roquefort, and Toasted Pecans on
Pain au Levain

This classic salad mixture makes a divine and oh so simple grilled cheese sandwich! Roquefort cheese is my ultimate French blue, with its saline flavor and the pungency that only a sheep's milk cheese seems to achieve. Spanish Cabrales is pretty wonderful, too, as are the American Point Reyes and Maytag blues. I would not use a rich and creamy blue such as Gorgonzola or Stilton in this sandwich, however, as it is pungency rather than creaminess that you want.

As for the red leaves, their slight bitterness is one of the best pairings with the richness and saltiness of blue veined cheeses. Radicchio, in fact, refers to a whole family of wonderful salad leaves. Red endive is beautiful, tasting just like a Belgian endive, and then there is Treviso, a long frond-like leaf with more fleshy rib and less leafy red. My favorite at the moment, though, is the Endiga, a little salad vegetable that combines the best of all of these, and it is so beautiful I can hardly bear for it to disappear into my mouth!

6–8 ounces Roquefort cheese

8 thin slices pain au levain or sourdough bread

About 3 tablespoons toasted coarsely chopped pecans

4–8 large leaves radicchio, or 8 to 12 leaves Treviso, red endive, or Endiga, as needed to fit the bread

Olive oil for brushing, or soft butter for spreading on bread

1 Spread the Roquefort cheese evenly on all 8 slices of bread.

2 Sprinkle 4 of the cheese-spread slices with pecans, then top each with a piece or 2 of the radicchio; use enough of the leaves to peek over the edges. Top each with a second piece of cheese-spread bread and press together to seal. Brush the outsides with the oil or butter.

3 Heat a heavy nonstick skillet or panini press over medium-high heat. Place the sandwiches in the pan, working in 2 batches, depending on size of the pan. Weight down according to the Tip on page 22, and cook, turning once or twice until the bread is crisp and the cheese has melted.

4 Serve immediately, cut into halves or quarters.

VARIATION *Gorgonzola and Basil* Tramezzini

The scent of basil is sooo alluring combined with creamy, pungent blue Gorgonzola. If Gorgonzola is not available, use Blue Castello instead. To make the sandwiches, substitute 8 ounces of Gorgonzola for Roquefort; add 2 to 3 whole leaves of sweet fresh basil per sandwich in place of radicchio. Omit the pecans, and proceed as directed above.

Totally Transylvanian:

Garlic Grilled Cheese on Rye

No vampire has a chance with the fragrant hit of garlic in these yummy sandwiches. Besides garlic in abundance, the sandwich has a zesty partnership of briny feta—sibling and soulmate to Rumanian brynza cheese—chopped onion, and a soft melting cheese, all sizzled atop rustic rye bread. Serve with Mediterranean Green Bean and Black Olive Salad (page 103) and a plate of sliced tomatoes, and pour yourself a nice cooling glass of lager.

4 large, thick slices of sourdough
  rye bread

4 cloves garlic, halved

4–6 ounces feta cheese, thinly sliced
  or crumbled

2 tablespoons chopped fresh
  chives or green onion

  About 6 ounces thinly sliced or
  shredded mild white melting
  cheese such as Jack, medium
  Asiago, or Chaume

1 Preheat the broiler.

2 Lightly toast the bread on a baking sheet under the broiler. Rub both sides with garlic. Chop any leftover garlic and set it aside for a moment.

3 Lay the feta over the top of the garlic-rubbed toasts, sprinkle with leftover chopped garlic, then with chives, and top with the second cheese.

4 Broil until the cheese melts and sizzles, lightly browning in spots, and the edges of the toast are crisp and brown.

5 Serve right away, hot and oozing.

4 slices hearty flavorful white or whole-wheat bread

About 3 tablespoons Bransten's Pickle, coarsely chopped if the fruit is in big pieces

6–8 ounces strong mature Cheddar cheese or English Cheshire, sliced

Cheese and pickle is a classic old-fashioned British sandwich, the sort you'd find in a motorway refreshment stop, a funky pub, greasy-spoon café, or school canteen. It's also a sandwich that many, many Brits dote on, whether they will admit it or not. Usually, the sandwich is eaten at room temperature, but toasting it transforms it deliciously.

Bransten's Pickle is not, as one might think, a pickled cucumber, but is actually a British institution—a sort of chutney-like, tangy (rather than hot), sweet puckery mixture of diced preserved vegetables (I believe rutabaga is a leading ingredient) with a decidedly tamarind flavor. Find Bransten's Pickle at specialty shops and supermarkets that sell British goodies; if it is either not available or not to your liking, choose a not-too-spicy chutney instead.

1 Preheat the broiler.

2 Arrange the bread on a baking sheet. Lightly toast under the broiler, then remove and spread the pickle generously on the lightly toasted bread; top with the cheese and pop under the broiler until the cheese melts.

VARIATION To make a pan-grilled cheese sandwich out of this, double the amount of bread and make the classic sandwich, then brown on both sides either in a skillet or in a panini press, until the cheese is melting and the bread toasty.

Comfy British Toasted Cheese:
Melted Cheese and Pickle

The streets of Paris are full of panini sellers offering up their delectable Franco-Italian sandwiches: Italian technique and spirit, luscious French cheeses such as local goat cheese . . . spiked with accents of olives, walnuts, tomatoes, or herbs. Buy one and eat it as you stroll the Marais, or go into the kitchen, put an Accordions of Paris CD on the player, and make yourself a goat cheese panino this instant!

If you have a panini press, as well as the soft smallish rolls—called, predictably, panini (i.e. "little breads")—that flatten out so perfectly into the distinctive Italian street sandwich, you will have a more authentic goodie. But if you don't, not a problem. Use a soft rather than crusty roll, as small as you can find, and remove about half of its bready filling. If you can't find a roll like this, use a pita bread instead. And I always think a nice panino is good with a bowl of Tomato Soup (page 104).

4 soft rolls, opened up and about half the bready interior pulled out

6–8 ounces spreadable or crumbly goat cheese (chèvre)

Olive oil for brushing bread

A WALNUT AND TOMATO CHÈVRE PANINI

2–3 medium to large tomatoes, thinly sliced

About ½ cup lightly toasted walnut pieces

B GREEN OLIVE AND THYME CHÈVRE PANINI

24–28 large green Greek olives, pitted and halved

A pinch of fresh or dried thyme

C GREEN CHILE AND CUMIN CHÈVRE PANINI

1 roasted, peeled, mild green chile (canned is fine)

1 clove garlic, chopped

A light sprinkle of ground cumin

1 Lay out the rolls and fill each one with 1½ to 2 ounces cheese, and one of the A, B, or C fillings. Close up and press together to seal well.

2 Heat a panini press and add the sandwiches, pressing as per directions. Or heat a heavy nonstick skillet over medium-high heat. Brush each sandwich lightly with olive oil, then add to the pan. Heat through, turning once or twice, until lightly crisped on the outside and the cheese is melted within.

3 Serve at once, cut into halves.

Three Panini
de Chèvre

Fresh Mozzarella, Prosciutto, and Fig Jam

4 soft French or Italian rolls (or half-baked if available)

10–12 ounces fresh mozzarella, thickly sliced

8 ounces prosciutto, thinly sliced

¼–½ cup fig jam or fig preserves, to taste

Soft butter for spreading on bread

Fresh milky mozzarella melts into a puddle of soothing, stringy cheese, with a hit of salty prosciutto, and a smudge of sweet fig jam to balance it all. For lunch, Spring Mix with Herbs (page 103) is nice alongside.

Fig jam and preserved figs, usually imported from Italy, Greece, or Turkey, are sometimes found in specialty shops and on Web sites as well as some supermarkets. If unavailable, use sliced fresh figs, drizzled with a tiny bit of honey.

1 Split each roll, and layer with the mozzarella and prosciutto. Spread the top slices with the fig jam, then close up.

2 Lightly butter the outside of each sandwich.

3 Heat a heavy nonstick skillet or panini press over medium-high heat. Place the sandwiches in the pan, working in two batches depending on the size of the pan. Press the sandwiches (see Tip, page 22) or close the grill and brown, turning once or twice, until the bread is crisp and the cheese has melted. Though the rolls start off as round, once pressed they are considerably flatter and can be easily turned, albeit carefully.

4 Serve right away, cut on the diagonal.

Panini Inglese: Rare Roast Beef with Blue Cheese and Watercress

4 soft sourdough or sweet rolls (or if available, 1 half-baked baguette, see page 18, cut into 4 portions)

10–12 ounces blue cheese, at room temperature for easier spreading

8–10 ounces rare roast beef, thinly sliced

Handful watercress leaves

Soft butter for spreading on bread

Salty, intensely aromatic blue cheese, rare lean beef, and the freshness of watercress leaves . . . this is a terrific sandwich that takes few ingredients, and only minutes to prepare. The combination of ingredients is English in inspiration, the technique is Italian street-food, the result: divine.

1 Split each roll, then spread generously with blue cheese on each side. Into each roll, layer the roast beef, then the watercress leaves, and close up again, pressing well to seal.

2 Lightly butter the outside of each sandwich.

3 Heat a heavy nonstick skillet, or panini press, over medium-high heat. Place the sandwiches in the pan, working in 2 batches, depending on the size of the pan. Weight down according to the Tip on page 22, and cook, turning once or twice until the bread is crisp and the cheese has melted.

4 Serve right away, cut on the diagonal.

Fresh Mozzarella, Prosciutto, and Fig Jam

Soft whole-wheat bread, thinly sliced onion, and red Leicester cheese, pressed and browned in the pan, until a little bit of the cheese melts out and crisps at the edges; the cheese is mild yet flavorful, melting with the onion into a perfect gooey cheese filling. It is so simple . . . but so good.

Accompany with your favorite mustard to dab into as you eat: I suggest a whole-grain mustard, or one green with herbs, such as Mustard with Shallot and Chives (page 105). Spicy Creole mustard is good, too. A handful of watercress on the side, and a cooling glass of beer . . . midnight snack perfection!

8 thin slices of soft whole wheat, sprouted wheatberry, dill, or hearty white such as potato bread

½ medium onion, peeled and very very thinly sliced crosswise

10–12 ounces red Leicester, Tillamook, or a mild Cheddar-type cheese

Olive oil for brushing or soft butter for spreading on bread

A mild, spunky, very interesting mustard of choice

1 Lay the slices of bread out. Top 4 pieces of bread with a single layer of onion, then enough cheese to cover the bread and onion completely. Top each with the remaining slices of bread to form sandwiches, and press together well.

2 Brush the outside of the sandwiches with olive oil or spread with soft butter.

3 Heat a heavy nonstick skillet or sandwich press over medium-high, then add the sandwiches and reduce the heat to medium. Place a weight on top (see Tip, page 22) if using a skillet, lowering the heat if it threatens to burn. Check every so often; when golden and flaked brown on one side, turn them over, weight down, and brown the second side.

4 Serve immediately, cut into wedges or triangles, accompanied by mustard for dabbing.

Red Leicester
with Onion

Spinach and Dill Havarti
on Multigrain Bread or Focaccia

Dill is always wonderful with spinach; here the dill oomphs up bland Havarti and is good melted between the covers of either multigrain bread or thick, squishy focaccia. The addition of spinach adds leafy freshness to the grilled cheese, and Sweet and Sour Roasted Peppers (page 104) add a bright accent. And, as long as you have extra dilled Havarti on hand, try also using it to make a Croque Monsieur with a Central European flavor: add a few slices of smoked ham, too!

2   cloves garlic, chopped

2   tablespoons extra-virgin olive oil, divided

1   cup cooked, chopped spinach, drained and squeezed dry

8   slices multigrain bread or 1 piece of focaccia, about 12 x 15 inches, cut horizontally

8   ounces dill Havarti, sliced

1 In a heavy nonstick skillet over medium-low heat, warm the garlic in 1 tablespoon of the olive oil, then add the spinach and cook together a moment or two to warm through.

2 On 4 slices of the bread (or the bottom layer of the focaccia), arrange the cheese, then top with the spinach and a second piece of bread (or the top of the focaccia). Press together to seal well, then lightly brush the outside of the sandwiches with the remaining olive oil.

3 Brown the sandwiches in the skillet, weighting them (see Tip, page 22), or in a panini press over medium-high heat. Cook until lightly crisped and golden on one side, then turn and brown the second side. When cheese is melted the sandwich is ready.

4 Serve immediately, cut on the diagonal.

4 slices good-quality white bread

6–8 ounces mature Cheddar cheese, thinly sliced

1–2 sweet gherkin or kosher dill pickles, thinly sliced

This is one of my glamorous Auntie Stelli's little tidbits she used to whip up when we were all kids. She still has a soft spot in her heart for these sandwiches, and I'm not sure if I dote on them because they are so tasty, or because I adore my aunt.

They take about 2 minutes to make. Though my aunt always used sweet pickle—the only time anyone in my family ate sweet pickle as we are still emphatically kosher dill people—any pickle is good in it. Made either way, the sandwich is delicious!

1 Preheat the broiler.

2 Lightly toast the bread under the broiler, then top each slice with a little cheese, the pickle, and more cheese. Broil until the cheese melts and the edges of the bread get crisp and browned.

3 Serve right away, cut into quarters.

Auntie Stelli's Open-Faced Grilled Cheddar and Dill Pickle

Harry's Bar Special, **PAGE 42**

Partytime Tidbits

Canapés, Crostini, and Bruschetta

Small individual grilled cheesy morsels are perfect celebration fare. Make a variety of goodies, serve a selection so that everyone gets to taste a variety of flavors and textures, and mix a jug of something refreshing. Voilà! Party time!

4

Harry's Bar Special

6 ounces Gruyère, Emmentaler, or other Swiss cheese, shredded coarsely

2–3 ounces diced smoked ham

A generous pinch of dry mustard

A few shakes of Worcestershire sauce

1 tablespoon whipping cream or sour cream, or enough to hold it all together

8 very thin slices of dense white bread, crusts cut off

Olive oil for brushing or soft butter for spreading on bread

Thin fingers of bread, crisp and golden, oozing a zesty cheese filling, are served with afternoon drinks at the legendary Harry's Bar. Pour yourself a glass of bubbly, nibble little sandwiches, and pretend you are in Venice. Served with an Arugula Salad (page 103), it makes a fine lunch or late-night supper.

The filling is a rich combination of shredded cheese with hits of mustard and Worcestershire for "zip," a dab of cream or sour cream a delicious liaison. Because the filling is so soft and squishy, the bread must be cut before assembling and cooking the sandwiches; slicing them after cooking makes the filling run out disastrously.

Trimming the crusts before cooking gives a crisper edge to the sandwich. If trimming the crusts and cutting the sandwiches into fingers seems a little too lah-de-dah, or a little too much effort, leave the crusts on, and cut the sandwiches into fetching little quarters from corner to corner instead of side to side.

1 In a medium bowl, combine the cheese with the smoked ham, mustard, and Worcestershire sauce. Mix well, then mix in the cream, adding just enough for it to form a firmish mixture and hold together.

2 Spread the cheese-and-ham mixture very thickly onto 4 pieces of the bread and top with the other 4. Press together well and cut sandwiches into 3 fingers each.

3 Brush the outside of the sandwiches with olive oil, then brown over medium-high heat in a heavy nonstick skillet, pressing them down using your spatula as they cook. When lightly crisped on the first side, turn them over and brown the second side.

4 Serve hot, right away.

This fragrant mixture of ricotta and mild Asiago cheeses, peppers, and pesto melts so seductively, you might find yourself using it to stuff into pastries or into chicken breasts. I've been wondering too what it would be like as a stuffing for cannelloni or ravioli.

16 thin baguette slices, cut on the diagonal and preferably a little stale

2 tablespoons extra-virgin olive oil

3 cloves garlic, minced, divided

4 ounces ricotta cheese

4 ounces mild Asiago, Jack, or fontina cheese, diced, shredded coarsely, or cut into strips

6–8 cherry tomatoes, quartered or diced

2 tablespoons chopped roasted red pepper

1–2 tablespoons basil pesto

1 Preheat the broiler.

2 Toss the baguette slices with the olive oil in a bowl, and arrange in a single layer in a baking dish or on a baking sheet. Toast under the broiler for about 5 minutes, or until lightly golden. Remove and toss the toasts with half of the garlic. Set aside.

3 In a small bowl, combine the remaining garlic with the ricotta cheese, Asiago, cherry tomatoes, peppers, and pesto.

4 Top each toast with a big dollop of the filling. Arrange on the baking sheet and pop under the broiler until the cheese melts and sizzles (especially the spots that melt onto the baking sheet and brown . . . mmmm . . . the best part), and the edges of the toasts crisp and brown.

5 Serve right away.

Crostini
alla Carnevale

Bruschetta from an Olive Grove in Puglia

We ate this almost every afternoon, with a glass of local wine or a fresh red wine and peach punch, for nearly a week as an afternoon pick-me-up at a rundown but breathtakingly elegant *agriturismo* (farm hotel) built around an old Baroque church. The weather was sultry and hovered over one hundred degrees every day, the greenery was lush and overgrown, and the setting of crumbling Baroque and rambling farm was Fellini-esque.

Bruschetta (pronounced: broo-sketta) is simply toasted country bread rubbed with garlic and drizzled with extra-virgin olive oil. Here it is topped with a layer of feta (in place of the local Italian cheese we enjoyed) and the surprise sunny accent of a grating of lemon rind, then sizzled under the grill until the cheese melts. A handful of arugula leaves on top adds freshness, and an Italian Tomato Salad (page 103) on the side makes lunch.

4 slices of pain au levain or other rustic country bread, cut into 4 to 6 pieces per slice

2 cloves garlic

About 1 tablespoon extra-virgin olive oil

4 ounces feta cheese, sliced

Grated zest of 1 lemon (unsprayed, see Note)

4 ounces mild melting cheese such as Jack, fontina, or mild Asiago, thinly sliced or shredded

About 3 ounces young arugula

1 Preheat the broiler.

2 Lightly toast the bread under the broiler. Remove from the heat and rub both sides with garlic.

3 Place the garlic-rubbed toasts on a baking sheet and drizzle very lightly with a little olive oil, then layer on the feta cheese, sprinkle with the lemon zest, top with the Jack cheese, and give a final drizzle of olive oil. Broil until the cheese melts and bubbles lightly.

4 Serve immediately, each tiny open-faced grilled cheese sandwich topped with a small handful of arugula leaves.

NOTE Since pesticides sprayed onto citrus remain on the skin, it's a good idea when eating the skin itself to choose unsprayed fruit.

Casse Croûte
of Blue Cheese and Gruyère
from the South of France

1 baguette, split lengthwise and slightly hollowed out

2–3 tablespoons soft butter for spreading on bread

1–2 tablespoons dry white wine

3–4 cloves garlic, chopped

8–10 ounces flavorful blue cheese such as Roquefort, Point Reyes blue, or *bleu d'Auvergne*, sliced or crumbled

8–10 ounces Gruyère or similar nutty "Swiss-type" cheese, such as Emmentaler, Comté, or Beaufort, thinly sliced

Grating of nutmeg

Casse croûte simply means a snack, usually a midmorning snack, especially one eaten in the field by workers such as those that tend the grapevines. Casse croûtes are usually accompanied by a glass—or two—of wine or something stronger. This snack is crusty bread, moistened with a few drops of wine, topped with a pungent blue cheese, then a layer of Gruyère, and broiled until melting. Accompany the casse croûtes with sweet Yellow Peppers and Basil (page 103) and enjoy them small for an appetizer, large for a supper or midnight snack . . . they are perfect any time.

1 Preheat the broiler.

2 Spread the baguette halves lightly on the inside with the butter, then sprinkle with some of the white wine and some of the garlic. Layer on the cheeses, ending with a layer of the Gruyère, and finishing with a grating of nutmeg, the remaining garlic, and a few drops more of the wine.

3 Broil the sandwiches until the cheese melts and sizzles and the edges of the bread crisp and brown.

4 Cut into pieces a few inches long, and serve right away.

SAUTÉED BLACK CHANTERELLES

1 ounce fresh or ½ ounce dried black chanterelle mushrooms

5–6 tablespoons unsalted butter

¼ cup mushroom or vegetable broth

1–2 tablespoons black truffle oil, or to taste

SANDWICHES

1 baguette (preferably 1 or 2 days stale), thinly sliced on a slight diagonal

8 ounces Comté cheese, sliced about ⅛-inch thick and cut to fit the small slices of baguette

1–2 tablespoons extra-virgin olive oil for brushing bread

1–2 cloves garlic, minced

1–2 tablespoons chopped fresh chives or flat-leaf parsley

This is inspired by a mid-winter cheese course served at the famed Paris restaurant L'Arpège. When our plates of aged Comté cheese were brought out, a big chunk of fresh black truffle was sitting next to it! The fragrance! The flavor! It was sublime.

Since fresh truffles are available only in winter, and even then, the farther you get from their source (France, Italy) the more prohibitively expensive they are, use a handful of sautéed and truffle-scented black chanterelle mushrooms, also known as *trompettes de la morte*, instead. Of course if you should be so lucky as to find a great cache of fresh black truffles, simply slice the truffle up, layer it with Comté cheese, and brown your little sandwiches into bliss.

1 To make the sautéed chanterelles: If using fresh mushrooms, wash and dry them, then chop finely. If using dried mushrooms, pour the mushroom broth, heated to just boiling, over the mushrooms to rehydrate. Leave to sit, covered, for about 30 minutes or until soft and pliable. Remove from the liquid and squeeze dry, reserving the liquid for the cooking below. Chop the rehydrated mushrooms and proceed as with fresh.

2 Heat the butter over medium heat in a heavy nonstick skillet; when melted and nutty brown, add the mushrooms and sizzle a few moments in the hot butter. Pour in the broth and cook over medium-high heat until the liquid is almost completely evaporated, 5 to 7 minutes. Remove from the heat and spoon into a bowl. Leave to cool a few minutes, then add the truffle oil, and stir well, mixing it in vigorously.

3 Lay out the baguette slices; smear half of them with the truffled mushroom mixture, then top with slices of the cheese and finally the remaining pieces of baguette. Press together well; the sandwiches, being small with a relatively dry filling, tend to fall apart. Once the sandwiches brown, however, the cheese melts and holds them together.

4 Brush the outside of each sandwich lightly with the olive oil. Heat a heavy nonstick skillet over medium-high heat and then add the sandwiches, working in batches as necessary. Top with a weight (see Tip, page 22) and reduce the heat to medium or medium-low. Brown the sandwiches, turning once or twice, until the bread is crisp and golden and the cheese has melted. Sprinkle with some of the garlic and chives, and serve.

5 Sprinkling on the garlic just before you remove it from the pan keeps the pungent and strong flavor of the raw garlic, so that each little sandwich tastes like a cheese-and-truffle-filled garlic crouton. Repeat with remaining sandwiches, removing any leftover garlic from the pan so it doesn't burn on the next round of sandwich browning.

Crisp Truffled Comté
with Black Chanterelles

Goat Cheese Toasts
with Desert Spices

12 thin baguette slices, preferably a little stale

Extra-virgin olive oil

3–4 ounces slightly aged (i.e. with a light crust) goat cheese such as Lezay, sliced about ½ inch thick and cut into pieces to fit the baguette slices

About ¼ teaspoon ground cumin

½ teaspoon thyme

¼–½ teaspoon paprika

About ⅛ teaspoon ground coriander

2 cloves garlic, chopped

1–2 tablespoons chopped fresh cilantro

Hot morsels of goat cheese on sesame toast, sprinkled with Middle Eastern spices, make this goat cheese nibble so fetching. The spice mixture approximates *za'atar*, a term that means "wild thyme," for that is an important ingredient; za'atar has come to refer to a blend of spices and nuts and/or seeds eaten in varying guises throughout the Eastern Mediterranean. Moroccan Carrot Relish (page 103) is nice alongside.

1 Preheat broiler.

2 Brush the baguette slices with olive oil, arrange in a single layer on a baking sheet, and lightly toast under the broiler on each side.

3 Top the toasted baguette slices with the cheese, then sprinkle with the cumin, thyme, paprika, coriander, and chopped garlic. Drizzle with olive oil and broil until the cheese melts slightly, and browns in spots.

4 Sprinkle with the cilantro and serve right away.

GINGERED BEET MARMALADE

3 medium-large red beets (16
   to 18 ounces total), whole and
   unpeeled

1 onion, quartered, plus ½ onion,
   chopped

½ cup red wine

   About ¼ cup red wine vinegar

   About 2 tablespoons sugar

2 tablespoons raisins or diced
   dried figs

   About ½-teaspoon chopped
   peeled fresh ginger

   Pinch of five-spice powder,
   cloves, or allspice

SANDWICHES

16 very thinly sliced diagonal pieces
   of stale baguette, or thinly sliced
   stale ciabatta

6 ounces Roquefort cheese

   About 1 tablespoon olive oil for
   brushing bread

   About 2 cups (3 ounces)
   watercress

These are crisp little slices of baguette filled with rich pungent Roquefort, and served with a dab of sweet savory beet marinade, with a tuft of fresh watercress to balance it all out. Serve as a first course or a light lunch, or serve a half portion (one little sandwich) as an appetizer or canapé.

The ginger beet marmalade makes more than you'll use in this recipe, but it's easiest to make a larger batch, as below. As it lasts a good week, or up to two months in the freezer, I'm sure you'll find delicious uses to put it to (starting with roast duck).

1 Preheat the oven to 375ºF.

2 *To make the beet marmalade:* Place the beets, quartered onion, and red wine in a baking pan just large enough to fit them with a few inches of space in-between. Cover the pan with aluminum foil, then bake for an hour, or until the beets are tender. Remove, uncover, and leave to cool.

3 When cool, slip the skin from the beets, then dice in ¼- to ⅛-inch pieces. Coarsely chop the cooked onion and combine it with the diced roasted beets and the cooking juices from the pan in a saucepan along with the chopped raw onion, vinegar, sugar, raisins, ginger, and several tablespoons of water. Bring to a boil and cook over medium-high heat until the onion is softened, and most of the liquid has evaporated. Do not let it burn. Remove from heat and adjust flavorings with more sugar and vinegar, for a decidedly sweet-sourish balance.

Season very subtly—a pinch only—with five-spice powder. Set aside. Makes about 2 cups.

4 *To make the sandwiches:* Lay out 8 of the baguette slices and spread each thickly with Roquefort cheese. Top each with the remaining slices of baguette and press together well to hold. Brush each side of the little sandwiches with a small amount of olive oil.

5 Heat a heavy nonstick skillet over medium-high heat and place the sandwiches in it. Reduce heat to medium-low or medium. Cook the sandwiches until they turn a crisp golden on the first side, press together lightly with the spatula, then turn and lightly brown the other side.

6 Serve the crisp hot little sandwiches on a plate, garnished with a tuft or two of watercress and a generous spoonful of the beet marmalade.

Crisp Little Roquefort Sandwiches
with Gingered Beet Marmalade

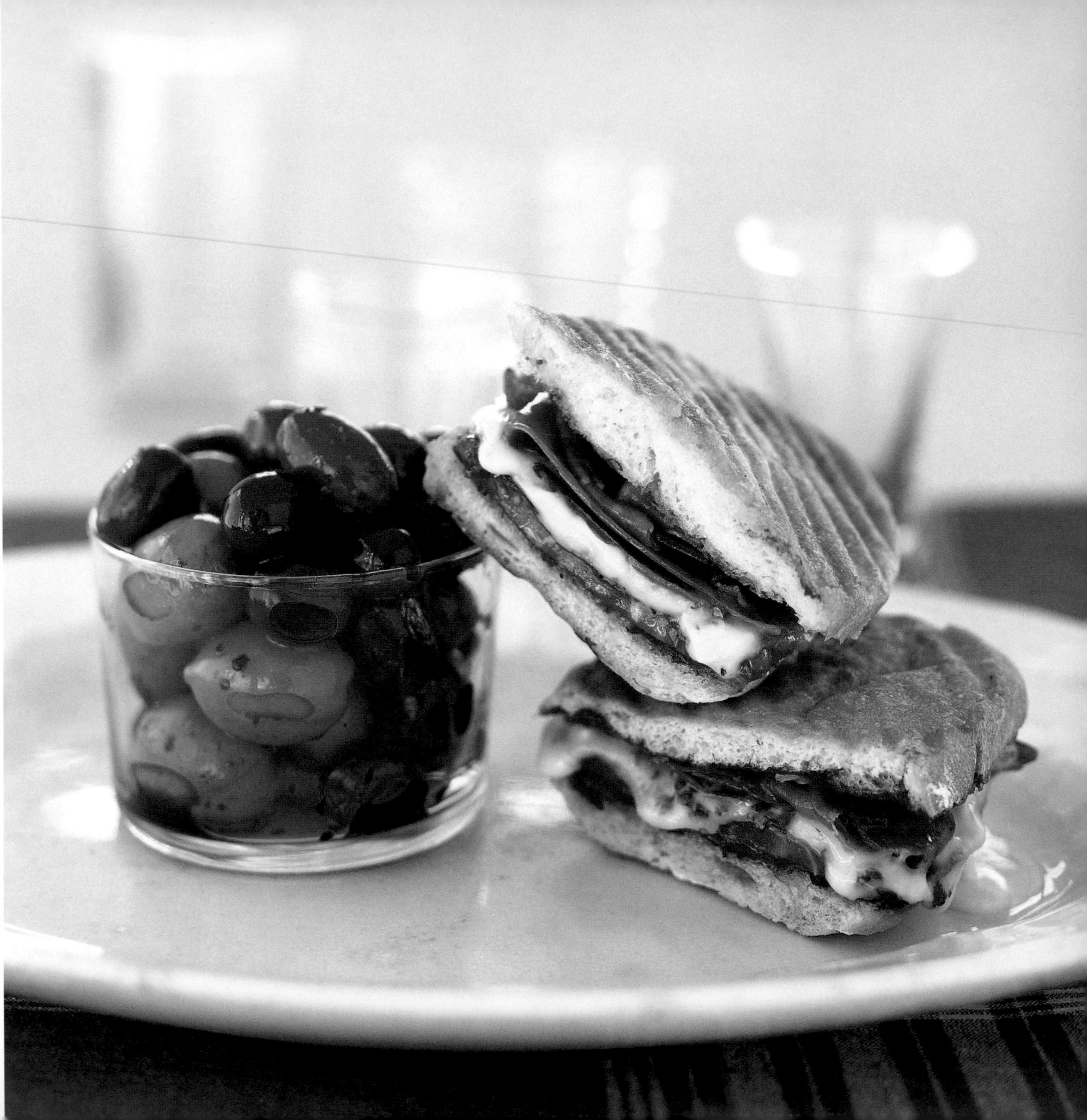

Bocadillo from the Island of Ibiza, PAGE 65

Classics and Twists

Cuban sandwiches, club sandwiches, and tuna melts—all classics, all delicious, all the more interesting when made with a flavor twist on the usual. Ordinary becomes extraordinary when the mayo is spiked with roasted peppers, the Cuban sandwich has *mojo* sauce, and the club is on pain au levain.

Tuna Melt

with Spanish Flavors

TUNA AND RED PEPPER SPREAD

- 6 ounces chunk white-meat tuna, packed in olive oil, drained
- 1 red pepper, roasted, peeled, and chopped (from a jar is fine)
- ½ onion, finely chopped
- 4–6 tablespoons mayonnaise
- 1 tablespoon extra-virgin olive oil
- 1–2 teaspoons paprika, preferably Hungarian or Spanish
- A few drops of fresh lemon juice
- Salt
- Black pepper

SANDWICHES

- 8 slices sun-dried tomato bread
- 8 ounces aged Gouda cheese, Jack, or white Cheddar
- Olive oil for brushing bread

This tuna melt is a kissin' cousin of the classic rainy-day lunch that you might have eaten—and still might eat—with tomato soup on a Saturday afternoon. Our tuna mixture is just a little different, inspired by a jar of tuna packed with roasted red peppers I picked up one day in Spain. Back in my home kitchen with no luscious Spanish tuna to enjoy, I approximated the mixture, starting with ordinary tuna steaks in olive oil, then adding roasted red pepper and paprika to oomph up the flavor. Then I slapped it onto sun-dried tomato bread with a fat slice of cheese. I've been slightly obsessed with tuna melt ever since. Whatever way the tuna melt is made, I always enjoy a plate of Zucchini and Summer Squash Bread-and-Butter Pickles (page 104) alongside.

1 To make the tuna mixture: Break up the tuna with a fork in a medium bowl, then mix with the red pepper, onion, mayonnaise, extra-virgin olive oil, paprika, lemon juice, salt, and pepper. Adjust amounts of mayonnaise to reach a nice thick consistency.

2 To make the sandwiches: Arrange 4 slices of the bread and top each with a quarter of the cheese. Top with the tuna mixture, then with the remaining bread.

3 Brush the outside of the sandwiches lightly with the olive oil. Heat a heavy nonstick skillet over medium-high heat and add the sandwiches. Weight them down with the bottom of a heavy frying pan (see Tip, page 22), not to press them but to hold the tops on and keep them flat while the cheese melts. Lower the heat to medium, and cook on the first side until the bread is crisp and golden, then turn over and repeat. Lift the weighting pan every so often to check on the situation with the cheese.

When it melts—and you can tell this because a little bit will ooze out—and the bread is gold and crisp, remove from the pan. If the bread is getting too dark before the cheese melts, reduce the heat.

4 Serve right away, hot and sizzling-crisp.

VARIATION *Griddled Crab, Avocado, Chipotle Chile, and Jack on Sourdough*

Use 6 ounces of drained crab in place of the tuna, and sourdough bread in place of the sun-dried tomato bread. Omit the roasted red pepper and paprika in the tuna mixture, and substitute 4 chopped green onions in place of the chopped onion. Include a layer of avocado in the sandwich, along with a shake or two of chipotle salsa such as Tabasco or Buffalo.

3 tablespoons mayonnaise
1 tablespoon capers, drained
8 thick slices bacon
8 thin slices pain au levain, cut from half a large loaf (about 10 inches long, 5 inches wide)
8 ounces Beaufort, Comté, or Emmentaler cheese, sliced

2 ripe tomatoes, sliced
2 poached, roasted, or grilled boneless chicken breasts, sliced
Olive oil for brushing bread
About 2 cups arugula leaves
About 12 leaves fresh basil

1 In a small bowl, combine the mayonnaise with the capers. Set aside.

2 Cook the bacon in a heavy nonstick skillet until it is crisp and brown on both sides. Remove from the pan and drain on absorbent paper towels.

3 Arrange 4 pieces of the bread on a work surface and top each with a layer of cheese, then a layer of tomatoes, bacon, and finally the chicken.

4 Generously spread the caper mayonnaise on the 4 remaining slices of bread and top each sandwich. Press to close tightly.

5 Brush the outsides lightly with olive oil.

6 Heat a heavy nonstick skillet or panini press over medium-high heat. Add the sandwiches, working in two batches if you need to. Weight down the sandwiches lightly (see Tip, page 22), reduce heat to medium, and cook until the bottom of the bread is browned in spots and the cheese has melted somewhat. Turn over carefully, using your hands to help stabilize the sandwiches on the spatula if they are threatening to fall apart. Brown on the second side, without a weight, but pressing on the sandwiches a bit to consolidate them and hold them together.

7 Remove from the pan, open the tops of all 4 sandwiches, and stuff in a handful of arugula and a few basil leaves, then close them all up.

8 Cut in halves and serve right away.

A club sandwich is, unlike your straightforward tuna melt or ham on rye, a posh little construction. While usually elegance is measured in restraint, a club sandwich knows no restraint yet nonetheless is the sandwich of choice of clubs and restaurants where conversation is muted and deals are done. Indeed, a club sandwich is too much of everything, a step beyond the BLT, a sandwich with everything inside *including* a BLT. This one is less towering and more manageable than the high stacks you find fastened together with decorated toothpicks. As a child I liked ordering a club sandwich just for the delight of deconstructing it and eating the various parts in whichever order I felt like, and of course, I loved those toothpicks!

As a grown-up I actually like it as below, all piled into one sandwich, browned and pressed into crisp plumpness. It's as classy as the original, but "down to earth" rather than wobbling and teetering in a ham, bacon, chicken, and melted cheesy tower. If you feel like rustling up a salad, too, make a Spring Mix with Herbs (page 103), on the side.

"Club Class" Sandwich

Great for brunch, lunch, or after-anything snack, here's a poached egg, topped with sharp and pungent Cheddar, mixed with a generous dash of Worcestershire sauce, then melted to sizzling cheesy yumminess. Omit the egg, if you like, for the British classic.

4	large eggs
	A few drops of white wine vinegar
4	slices whole-wheat or sourdough bread, or 2 halved English muffins
	About 2 tablespoons soft butter
12	ounces sharp Cheddar or Cheshire cheese, coarsely shredded
1–2	green onions, thinly sliced
1–2	teaspoons ale or lager (optional)
½	teaspoon whole-grain mustard and/or several pinches powdered dry mustard
	Several generous shakes of Worcestershire sauce
	Several shakes of cayenne pepper

1 Poach the eggs: Crack each egg and place in a cup or ramekin. Bring a deep skillet filled with water to a boil; lower the heat and keep it at a bubbling simmer. Do not salt the water, but rather, add a few shakes of vinegar. Slip each egg into the lightly simmering water. Because of the vinegar, the whites should firm up rather than run uncontrollably. Cook the eggs until the whites are firmish and the yolks still runny, 2 to 3 minutes. Remove with a slotted spoon and place on a plate to drain excess water.

2 Preheat the broiler.

3 Lightly toast the bread under the broiler and lightly butter it.

4 Arrange the bread on a baking sheet. Top each piece with 1 of the poached eggs.

5 In a medium bowl, mix together the Cheddar, green onions, ale, mustard, Worcestershire sauce, and cayenne pepper. Gently spoon the cheese mixture evenly over the poached eggs, taking care not to break the yolks.

6 Broil the cheese-and-egg-topped toasts until the cheese melts into a gooey saucelike mixture, and the edges of cheese and toast alike crisp and brown. Serve right away.

Welsh Rarebit
with Poached Egg

Austin Powers'
Shag-a-delic

1970s Grilled Ham, Cheese, and Pineapple

6–8 ounces turkey ham, coarsely chopped or cut into ribbons if already thinly sliced

3 tablespoons mayonnaise or as needed

4 thick slices fresh pineapple or 5 slices canned in its own juice (if using fresh, a small sprinkle of sugar may be necessary)

8 slices whole-wheat or wheatberry bread, thinly sliced

About 12 to 15 slices of bread-and-butter pickles or 8 to 10 Peppadew Piquanté Peppers

½ onion, thinly sliced

About 8 ounces Taleggio cheese (rind cut off), or sharp Cheddar cheese, sliced

Extra-virgin olive oil for brushing bread

Get out your shag-pile carpet, kick off your shoes, and dance the "funky chicken" for all you're worth. Then hunker down and melt yourself some cheese sandwiches in the theme of the '70s: ham, cheese, and pineapple. Fancy decorated toothpicks holding them together are optional.

Update for modern times: I've used turkey ham in place of the pork variety. And for sophistication, a layer of Taleggio cheese, but a nice sharp Cheddar is also good in its place, although very different.

If you can find the brand of little sweet-spicy peppers called Peppadew Piquanté Peppers, include them in this sandwich. Otherwise any sweet-sour-spicy ones will do, such as bread-and-butter pickles.

1 In a small bowl, combine the turkey ham with the mayonnaise. Set it aside.

2 Dice or coarsely chop the pineapple and set it aside in a bowl. If using fresh, toss it with sugar to taste.

3 Lay out the bread slices. On 4 of them spread the pineapple. On the other 4, first place some of the pickles, then the turkey ham salad mixture, then some onion, and the Taleggio. Carefully top with the pineapple-topped bread slices to form sandwiches, and press together tightly. Brush each side lightly with the olive oil.

4 Heat a heavy nonstick skillet or panini press over medium-high heat. Place the sandwiches in the pan, browning and pressing, until the first side is crisp and golden and the cheese begins to melt; then using your spatula and possibly a little help from your hand, carefully turn the sandwiches over and cook on the second side, pressing as they brown.

5 When the sandwiches are crisp and lightly browned on both sides and the cheese is melted, remove from pan, cut into halves, and serve (this is a messy sandwich, so get prepared to lick the delicious goo from your fingers).

A Hot Muffaletta

Muffaletta is a Naw Ahleeens sandwich—a sandwich that is as loud and snappy with its flavors as is the legendary night life of New Orleans itself. While it's usually eaten cold, the cheese, vinaigrette, and other goodies make this an especially good sandwich for heating and grilling. And this muffaletta has an extravagance of everything: dripping melted cheese, reeking of garlic and the scent of salami, soaked with olive oil, and fragrant with oregano. Extras only add allure; here we try pickled peppers, capers, and roasted peppers.

Mortadella is, for anyone not aware of it, the big pink white-flecked bologna-like cold cut you see in deli cases; sometimes it's speckled with black peppercorns, other times with pale green pistachio nuts. Mortadella is mild and aromatic with a tender, slightly bouncy texture, and it's one of the most sumptuous cold cuts you could treat yourself to. A little Mediterranean Green Bean and Black Olive Salad (page 103) makes a muffaletta into a meal.

- 4 soft French rolls
- Extra-virgin olive oil
- A few shakes here and there of red wine vinegar
- 4–6 cloves garlic, chopped
- 3–4 teaspoons capers, drained
- 2–3 large pinches of dried oregano, crumbled
- ½ cup chopped or diced roasted red pepper
- 4 mild pickled peppers, such as Greek or Italian, sliced
- ½ red or other mild onion, very thinly sliced
- ½ cup pimiento-stuffed green olives, sliced
- 1 large tomato, thinly sliced
- 4 ounces dried salami, thinly sliced
- 4 ounces Westphalian ham, smoked turkey, or mortadella
- 8 ounces thinly sliced provolone cheese

1 Open the rolls and pull out a bit of their fluffy insides. Sprinkle each cut side with olive oil and vinegar, then with the garlic, capers, and oregano. On 1 side of each roll, layer the red pepper, pickled peppers, onion, olives, tomato, salami, ham, and finally the cheese. Close up tightly and press together well to help seal.

2 Heat a heavy nonstick skillet over medium-high heat and lightly brush the outside of each roll with olive oil. Place the sandwiches in the pan and weight down (see Tip, page 22), or place them in a panini press. Cook until golden brown on one side, then turn and brown the second side. Sandwiches are ready when they are crisply golden and the cheese has oozed a bit and crisped in places. Cut into halves, and eat right away.

MOJO SAUCE

- 2 tablespoons extra-virgin olive oil
- 8 cloves garlic, thinly sliced
- 1 cup fresh orange juice and/or grapefruit juice
- ½ cup fresh lime juice and/or lemon juice
- ½ teaspoon ground cumin
- Salt
- Black pepper

SANDWICHES

- 1 soft baguette or 4 soft long French rolls, split
- Soft butter or olive oil for brushing bread
- 6 ounces thinly sliced boiled or honey-roast ham
- 1 cooked chicken breast, about 6 ounces, thinly sliced
- 8 ounces flavorful cheese such as Gouda, manchego, or Edam, sliced
- 1 dill, kosher dill, or sweet pickle, thinly sliced
- About 4 leaves butter or Boston Bibb lettuce
- 2–3 medium, ripe tomatoes, sliced

A friend went to Cuba, then came to visit me in London, awash with big passion for the delicious flattened sandwiches from Cuba. These sandwiches are much like Italian panini, but filled with a Latin American burst of flavor and ingredients. Later, when we worked together on a book about Florida, we found ourselves in the kitchen for hours on end whipping up our own versions and variations (in the name of research, of course, as Miami is full of cafés specializing in Cuban sandwiches. I repeat, it had nothing to do with greed).

This recipe includes *mojo* sauce, a vinaigrette based on citrus juice instead of vinegar. It makes about 1½ cups mojo sauce, which is more than you'll need for these sandwiches; this gives you the delicious bonus of leftovers, which will enhance almost anything barbecued: lamb, beef, chicken, fish, or shellfish. Moroccan Carrot Relish (page 103) is good alongside.

Cuban Sandwich
via London and Miami

1 To make the Mojo Sauce: Gently heat the olive oil and garlic in a small heavy skillet until the garlic is lightly golden but not browned, about 30 seconds. Add the citrus juices, cumin, salt, and pepper to taste, and remove from the heat. Let cool, taste, and adjust for seasoning. Lasts up to 3 days in the refrigerator. Makes 1½ cups.

2 Preheat the broiler.

3 To make the sandwiches: Pull out a little of the fluffy insides of each roll. Discard the pulled out bread or reserve it for another use. Brush both sides of the rolls with a small amount of soft butter or olive oil. Lightly toast under the broiler on each side, then remove from the heat.

4 Splash a little of the mojo sauce onto the cut sides of the bread, then layer with the ham, chicken, cheese, and pickle. Close up well and press together to help seal and lightly brush outsides of the sandwiches with olive oil.

5 Heat a heavy nonstick skillet or panini press over medium-high heat, and brown the sandwiches, weighting them down (see Tip, page 22). You want to press the sandwiches as flat as possible. Cook until lightly crisped on the outside and the cheese begins to melt. Squish the sandwiches with the spatula when you turn them to help press them flat, too. (You can bake these sandwiches instead of frying them: wrap the sandwiches in foil and place on a baking sheet. Top with a second baking sheet and a heavy weight. Bake in a 400°F oven for about 10 minutes, or until the sandwiches are browned and crisp.)

6 When sandwiches are crisp and browned, remove from the pan. Open up, add the lettuce and tomato, and serve right away, with extra mojo on the side.

Croque Monsieur is *the* nibble of the cafés and wine bars of France. Each establishment has its own; some versions are unfortunately pedestrian, some gloriously delicious. At its essence, croque monsieur is a ham sandwich that is broiled, then topped with cheese (grated cheese gives a nice crisp and lacey edge to the cheese topping). A decade or two back, it was always topped with béchamel sauce before the cheese, and sometimes it was all dipped into egg and browned in the pan, a veritable ham and cheese–stuffed French toast. These days the sandwiches vary wildly from café to café.

All you need with any croque, whether it is monsieur, compagnarde, madame, etc., is a fresh-leafed crisp little salad alongside, such as the Paris Café Salad of greens and beets (page 103).

8 slices firm, flavorful good-quality white or French bread

4 thin slices boiled or baked ham or turkey ham

2 tablespoons unsalted soft butter

4 ounces Gruyère-type cheese, or similar cheese such as Emmentaler or Appenzell, grated

1 Preheat the broiler.

2 Arrange 4 slices of the bread on a baking sheet, then top with the ham and the remaining slices of bread to make sandwiches. Butter each sandwich on the outside, then place under the broiler until lightly golden, turn, and brown on the second side.

3 Sprinkle cheese all over the top of one side of the sandwiches, then return to the broiler for a few moments or until the cheese melts and bubbles a bit here and there. Eat right away with green salad nestled next to it.

VARIATIONS

Croque Madame: Parisian Ham and Cheese Sandwich with an Egg Prepare as above, making the ham sandwiches and toasting on each side. Before you add the cheese, however, cut a circle in the top of each sandwich through the top piece of bread only, exposing the ham within. Lay these rounds of toast out on the baking sheet next to the sandwiches and sprinkle their tops with the cheese. Into the hollows that you've cut in each sandwich, break an egg and slide it right into the indentation of the bread, and onto the ham. Sprinkle cheese over the egg as well; dot with a little butter and broil until the egg white sets, the yolk is still very runny, and the cheese is melted. Serve each sandwich with the cheese-topped round of bread at an angle, propped up against the egg, exposing the egg.

Croque Señor: Use country bread such as a pain au levain instead of delicate white. Substitute a dried Spanish chorizo sausage (much like pepperoni or one of the spicy Italian salamis from Calabria—i.e. a chorizo that has big flavor but does not need cooking) in place of the ham, and manchego or Idiazábal cheese instead of the Emmentaler or Appenzell.

Croque Monsieur
et Sa Famille:
A Whole Family of Parisian Grilled Cheese

Bocadillo from the Island of Ibiza

4 large soft flattish French or Italian-style rolls, preferably sourdough

6–8 cloves garlic, halved

4–6 tablespoons extra-virgin olive oil

1 tablespoon tomato paste (optional)

2–3 large ripe tomatoes, thinly sliced

Generous sprinkling of dried oregano (preferably Greek, Sicilian, or Spanish)

8 thin slices Spanish *jamon* or similar ham such as prosciutto

About 10 ounces mild and melting, yet flavorful cheese, such as manchego, Idiazábal, Mahon, or a California cheese such as Ig Vella's semi secco or Jack

Mixed Mediterranean olives

Bocadillos are grilled sandwiches from Ibiza, the Mediterranean island that is part Spain, part nightlife and clubbing, and part Marin County in its ambience. A large part of Ibiza's identity is its hippie and artistic population; it's an island where hippie and artist expats from Northern Europe and California, refugees from the '60s, and their followers have melded with the Spanish population and formed a unique culture awash in tie-dye and tapas. There is a constant influx of artists coming and going and keeping everything more interesting and lively— often too much so!

This particular *bocadillo* was my favorite: rubbed with garlic, moistened with olive oil, and full of tomatoes, ham, and melted cheese. We often trotted down to the nearby village of Santa Gertrudis where, from early morning to late night, the espresso machine would hiss, and the toaster would issue these nearly addictive morsels. We'd order a *bocadillo* and eat it out on the patio. Village life paraded past us, and as we munched and gazed and sipped, we fed little bites to the various cats and dogs who inevitably gathered around our feet begging for morsels.

1 Preheat the broiler.

2 Cut open the rolls and lightly toast on each side under the broiler.

3 Rub the garlic on the cut side of each piece of bread. (I chop any leftover garlic to sprinkle onto the cheese, but this is optional and untraditional.)

4 Drizzle the garlic-rubbed bread with the olive oil and brush the outsides with a bit more of the oil. Spread lightly with the tomato paste, then layer the sliced tomatoes and their juices onto the rolls, pressing in the tomato paste and tomatoes so that the juices are absorbed into the bread. Sprinkle with crumbled oregano, then layer with the ham and cheese. Close up and press together well, then brush lightly with olive oil.

5 Heat a heavy nonstick skillet pan or panini press over medium-high heat, then add the sandwiches. If using a pan, weight the sandwiches down (see Tip, page 22). Lower the heat to medium-low and cook until lightly crisped on the outside and the cheese begins to melt. Turn over and brown on the second side.

6 Cut in halves, and serve immediately, with a handful of mixed olives alongside.

Mediterranean Meltdown: Ripe Tomato, Mahon Cheese, and Fresh Thyme on Black Olive Bread, PAGE 70

Simple, Sensational

Basic Grilled Cheese with a Little Something Extra

A sprinkling of fresh herbs, a thin layer of fruit, a dab of rich sauce, or a crunch of fragrant spice seeds: these are all basic old-fashioned grilled cheese sandwiches with a little something extra added.

Saltimbocca Sandwich

10–12 fresh, small sage leaves

3 tablespoons unsalted butter

1 tablespoon extra-virgin olive oil

8 slices country bread

4 ounces prosciutto, thinly sliced

10–12 ounces full-flavored mountain cheese such as fontina, aged Beaufort, or Emmentaler

2 cloves garlic, chopped

A classic combination of prosciutto, cheese, and sage fills this sandwich with the flavors of the Roman classic, saltimbocca, in which the goodies stuff or top thin scallopine of veal, chicken, or turkey. An invigorating Whole Endive Leaf Salad (page 103) makes a bright counterpoint to the rich sandwich.

1 In a heavy nonstick skillet, stir the sage leaves, butter, and olive oil together over medium-low heat until the butter melts and foams.

2 Meanwhile, lay out 4 slices of bread, top with the prosciutto, then the fontina, then a sprinkle of garlic. Place the remaining bread on top and press together firmly.

3 Gently place the sandwiches in the hot sage-butter mixture; you may need to do them in several batches or use 2 pans. Weight with a heavy frying pan on top (see Tip, page 22) to press the sandwiches down. Cook until lightly crisped on the outside and the cheese begins to melt. Turn over and brown on the second side.

4 Serve sandwiches hot and crisp, cut into diagonal halves. Either discard the sage leaves or nibble them up, crisp and browned.

Melted Appenzell, Emmentaler, Pear, and Cumin

8 thin slices pain au levain, sourdough, or sour pumpernickel

4 ounces Emmentaler cheese, thinly sliced

1 ripe but firm pear, unpeeled and very thinly sliced

4 ounces Appenzell cheese, thinly sliced

Several pinches of cumin seeds

Soft butter or olive oil for brushing bread

Wafer-thin pear slices add a sweet, tart, and juicy accent to this rich mixture of Swiss cheeses and earthy cumin seed. Use any cheese from Switzerland or the Jura (France) with a good strong flavor. For a more Dutch flavor, choose Edam or Gouda instead.

1 Arrange 4 slices of the bread on a work surface, then top with a layer of the Emmentaler cheese, then the pear, then some Appenzell cheese, and a sprinkling of cumin seeds. Top each sandwich with a second slice of bread and press together firmly to seal.

2 Spread the outside of each sandwich lightly with butter. Heat a heavy nonstick skillet or sandwich press over medium-high heat. Put a weight on the sandwiches (see Tip, page 22). Brown, turning once or twice, until the bread is crisp and golden and the cheese has melted. Serve right away.

Grilled Pumpernickel and Gouda

with Parsley-Tarragon Mustard

Nutty aged Gouda, manchego, a semi-dry Jack, or medium Asiago are all good cheeses in this sandwich. Soft pumpernickel is as fetching for its dark brown-black color as it is for its earthy flavor, but a nice sourdough or whole-wheat bread studded with grain kernels is delicious too. A bowl of Tomato Soup (page 104) would be good alongside. You might want to make a double batch of the easily prepared herbed mustard; it is delicious on almost any grilled or steamed sausage, or slathered onto a rare roast beef sandwich.

PARSLEY-TARRAGON MUSTARD

3 tablespoons whole-grain mustard

3 tablespoons mild Dijon mustard

2 tablespoons chopped fresh flat-leaf parsley

1 tablespoon chopped fresh tarragon

1 small clove garlic, minced

A few drops of red or white wine vinegar, to taste

SANDWICHES

8 slices soft dark pumpernickel bread

8 ounces aged Gouda, manchego, or similar nutty aged cheese

Soft butter or olive oil for brushing bread

1 To make the Parsley-Tarragon Mustard: Combine the whole-grain and Dijon mustards in a small bowl and stir in the parsley, tarragon, and garlic. Add a few drops of vinegar to taste and set aside. Makes about 1/3 cup.

2 To make the sandwiches: Arrange 4 slices of the bread on a work surface. Add a layer of the cheese, then top with the second piece of bread. Press together and lightly spread or brush the outsides with the butter.

3 Heat a heavy nonstick skillet or panini press over medium-high heat and add the sandwiches. Weight with a second frying pan (see Tip, page 22) and reduce the heat to medium-low. Cook until the first side is crisp and golden, then turn and cook the second side until the cheese is melted.

4 Serve immediately, with the Parsley-Tarragon Mustard on the side, to dab on as desired.

Mediterranean Meltdown

Ripe Tomato, Mahon Cheese, and Fresh Thyme on Black Olive Bread

8 slices black olive bread
1 clove garlic, finely chopped
4 big, fat, ripe, flavorful tomatoes
1–2 teaspoons fresh thyme leaves
8–10 ounces Mahon, aged Gouda, or Mezzo Secco cheese
Olive oil for brushing bread

Mahon is a Gouda-like cheese from the Spanish island of Minorca; it makes gorgeous melted sandwiches with the ripe tomatoes of summer. Gouda or a flavorful manchego would both be good substitutes, but if you have the opportunity, enjoy Mezzo Secco on this sandwich. It's a lightly aged Jack cheese, halfway flavor- and texture-wise between milky mild Sonoma Jack and the nutty dry Jack used for grating. Mezzo Secco is made only by Vella Cheese Company, a legendary cheesemaker in Sonoma, California.

If black olive bread is unavailable, simply use sourdough and add a scattering of halved black Mediterranean-style olives to the sandwich filling.

1 Sprinkle 4 of the slices of bread with the garlic, then layer with the tomatoes (allow their juices to sink into the bread). Sprinkle the tomato slices with the thyme leaves. Top with a layer of the cheese, then the remaining bread, to form 4 sandwiches. Press together to seal well. Brush the outsides of each with the olive oil.

2 Heat a heavy nonstick skillet or sandwich press over medium-high heat and add the sandwiches, weighting them down (see Tip, page 22). Brown the sandwiches, turning once or twice, until the bread is crisp and golden and the cheese has melted, oozing out and crisping just a little as it hits the pan.

3 Serve right away.

Smoked Turkey, Taleggio, Gorgonzola and Apple

1 soft, flat, airy Italian bread, such as ciabatta, or 4 soft Italian/French rolls; if half-baked are available, choose these

6 ounces Gorgonzola cheese, thinly sliced or crumbled coarsely

8 ounces smoked turkey, thinly sliced

1 medium or 2 small crisp but flavorful apples, cored, unpeeled, and very thinly sliced

6 ounces Taleggio, Teleme, Jack, or a tomme de montagne cheese, cut into 4 slices (Whether to leave the Taleggio rind or cut it off is up to you; the rind has a slightly strong flavor which some love, some emphatically do not.)

Olive oil for brushing bread

A delightful sandwich, and the essence of ease itself to whip up. The melted Taleggio is soft and gooey, and along with the rich and pungent Gorgonzola, is accented by the savory, smoky turkey and the sweet/tart juiciness of apple. Arugula Salad (page 103) is nice and fresh alongside.

1 Cut the bread into 4 equal-sized pieces. Slice each piece of bread horizontally, leaving 1 side connected if possible.

2 Open up the 4 pieces of bread. On 1 side layer the Gorgonzola, smoked turkey, and sliced apple in equal amounts. Top with the Taleggio and close the sandwiches up tightly, pressing firmly to close.

3 Brush the sandwiches, top and bottom, with olive oil, then heat a heavy nonstick skillet over medium-high heat. Place the sandwiches in the hot pan and reduce the heat at once to very low. Weight on top (see Tip, page 22), or use a sandwich press or panini press.

4 Cook until they are golden brown and toasted, then turn over and lightly brown the second sides. Check every so often to be sure that the bread is not burning.

5 Serve as soon as both sides are crisp and the cheese is melted.

Rosemary-Scented Melted Jarlsberg and Red Pepper on Sourdough

8 medium-thick slices sourdough bread

8 ounces Jarlsberg or a mild melting cheese such as Jack

2 roasted red peppers, sliced, or 3 to 4 tablespoons chopped roasted red peppers

2 cloves garlic, thinly sliced

2 teaspoons chopped fresh rosemary leaves, or to taste

Olive oil for brushing bread

This simple sandwich makes you remember why you loved grilled cheese so much as a kid: it's crisp, rich, zesty, and comforting. The enticing aroma of garlic and rosemary helps you remember you're not a kid anymore.

1 Arrange 4 slices of bread on a work surface and top with the cheese, then add the red peppers, garlic, and rosemary. Top with the remaining slices of bread and press together gently. Brush the outside of each sandwich lightly with the oil.

2 Heat a heavy nonstick skillet or sandwich press over medium-high heat and add the sandwiches, working in several batches if need be. Lower the heat to medium-low, browning the sandwiches slowly (press with the spatula to help crisp), until lightly crisped on the outside and the cheese begins to melt. Turn over and repeat on second side.

3 Serve each sandwich cut into halves or quarters.

Hot Torta of Chicken, Green Chile, Queso Fresco, and Gouda, PAGE 76

Extravaganzas

Sometimes a grilled cheese sandwich is more than a grilled cheese sandwich. For example, occasionally the layers of bread and cheese demand embellishment — say, a layer of sautéed wild mushrooms, a slick of truffle paste, a sprinkling of diced preserved lemons. Sometimes a grilled cheese sandwich yearns to be cloaked in a rich and creamy mushroom sauce, a sautéed slice of turkey or chicken or sausage, or a homemade chipotle chile salsa . . . sometimes a grilled cheese sandwich becomes, in fact, an extravaganza. It's still a grilled cheese sandwich, mind you, but now it's a big delicious deal!

Sage Sausage and Jack Cheese

with Shreds of Preserved Lemon

2 sage/herbed sausages (about 14 ounces), either pork, turkey, or vegetarian

6 ounces shredded Jack or medium Asiago cheese

1–2 tablespoons (about 2 ounces) freshly grated aged cheese such as Parmesan, locatelli Romano, or dry Jack

2 green onions, thinly sliced

2–3 teaspoons sour cream

Pinch of cumin seeds

Tiny pinch of turmeric

Dab of brown mustard

Pinch of cayenne pepper or a few drops hot pepper sauce

8 thin slices whole-grain (such as wheatberry, sunflower seed, or sprouted wheat) bread

2–3 tablespoons extra-virgin olive oil

3 cloves garlic, thinly sliced

1–2 Moroccan-style preserved lemons, rinsed well and sliced into slivers or chopped

1–2 teaspoons finely chopped fresh flat-leaf parsley

These may sound like unusual ingredients to combine—Mediterranean sage, cheese, and the tangy preserved lemons of North Africa—yet they work together deliciously. The various spices enhance the cheese, and the shreds of salty lemon give a sprightly, bright contrast to the herby sausage. Preserved lemons are eaten in Moroccan and other Middle Eastern cuisines and sometimes can be found in shops catering to these cultures. They are also very simple to make yourself: most Moroccan cookbooks will provide you with a good reliable and easy recipe. As for the sausage, any sage sausage may be used: pork, turkey, or vegetarian.

Serve this sandwich cut into triangles to go with drinks—in fact, if you have a sandwich maker that presses and seals the edges while it grills, this is a good sandwich to make in it.

1 Roughly dice the sausages, then brown them quickly over medium heat in a small nonstick skillet. Remove from the pan, place on paper towels, and leave to cool. Leave the pan on the stove and turn off the heat.

2 In a medium bowl, mix together the 2 cheeses with the green onions, sour cream, cumin seeds, turmeric, mustard, and cayenne pepper. When the sausage is cool, mix it into the cheese.

3 Pile 4 slices of the bread with the cheese-and-sausage mixture, then top with a second piece of bread. Pat down well and press lightly but firmly so that the sandwich will hold together.

4 Reheat the pan over medium-high heat and add about half the olive oil and garlic, then push the garlic to one side and add 1 or 2 sandwiches, however many the pan will hold. Cook until lightly crisped on one side and the cheese begins to melt. Turn over and cook the second side until it is golden brown. Remove to a plate and repeat with the other sandwiches, garlic, and oil. You may either discard the lightly browned garlic or nibble on it; whichever you do, remove it from the pan before it blackens as it will give a bitter flavor to the oil if it burns.

5 Serve the sandwiches right away, piping hot, cut into triangles, and sprinkled with the preserved lemon and chopped parsley.

Tortas are a Mexican sandwich, filled with all sorts of spicy taco fillings such as beans and grilled or stewed meats, and spiked with salsa, but sandwiched into a chunky roll instead of a tortilla. Tortas are Mexican street food par excellence—you see signs on the streets everywhere announcing what's on offer at this street stand, that café, this marketplace.

Our filling here: juicy chicken breast, earthy roasted chiles, milky *queso fresco*, and rich melted Gouda just need a dab of tangy green tomatillo salsa to make a deliciously messy, irresistible meal in a sandwich.

Four 5- to 6-ounce boneless skinless chicken breasts, lightly pounded to flatten

1 tablespoon fresh lemon juice

1 tablespoon cornstarch

2 cloves garlic, chopped

Salt

Black pepper

2 green chile peppers (or one 6-ounce can roasted mild green chiles)

3 tablespoons extra-virgin olive oil, or as needed

4 soft sourdough rolls, halved

Green tomatillo salsa

Large pinch of cumin seeds

6 ounces queso fresco, sliced

6 ounces mild yet flavorful cheese such as Gouda, manchego, or Jack, sliced

4 tablespoons sour cream

1 In a shallow bowl, combine the chicken with the lemon juice, cornstarch, garlic, salt, and black pepper. Set aside.

2 Roast the chile peppers over an open fire or under a broiler until they blister and char evenly. Rinse under cold running water as you peel off the skin; remove stems and seeds and slice the peppers into fat strips.

3 In a heavy nonstick skillet, add 2 tablespoons of the olive oil, and over medium-high heat brown the chicken breasts first on one side, then another. Cook only about 2 minutes per side, pressing them with a heavy object such as a pan lid (see Tip, page 22) while they brown. Remove from the pan and set aside while you assemble the sandwiches.

4 Open each roll and brush the outsides with olive oil. On each roll, spread a spoonful of green tomatillo salsa, then layer a chicken breast, pepper strips, a sprinkling of cumin, queso fresco, and Gouda; top with a slather of sour cream and then close up.

5 Heat the same pan over medium-high heat and place the sandwiches in the pan, then reduce the heat to medium-low. Weight down the sandwiches gently. Brown them, turning once or twice, until the bread is golden in spots and the cheese has melted.

6 Serve the sandwiches with additional green tomatillo salsa on the side.

VARIATION *Black Bean and Two-Cheese Tortas*

Substitute 1 to 1½ cups refried black beans (from a can is fine) for the cooked chicken breast, and add a handful of shredded lettuce when the tortas come hot from the pan.

Hot Torta
of Chicken, Green Chile, Queso Fresco, and Gouda

Panini of
Eggplant
Parmigiana

¼ cup extra-virgin olive oil, or as desired, divided

1 medium eggplant, sliced ½ to ¾ inch thick

Salt

4 large softish rolls, sourdough or sweet

3 cloves garlic, chopped

8 big fresh basil leaves

About ½ cup ricotta cheese

3 tablespoons freshly grated Parmesan, pecorino, or locatelli Romano cheese

6–8 ounces fresh mozzarella cheese

4 ripe juicy tomatoes, thinly sliced (including their juices)

Browned eggplant slices, with a hit of ripe tomato, and the smell of garlic lurking everywhere, this sandwich is like an eggplant parmigiana in a roll. Treat yourself to an Arugula Salad (page 103), too—delish.

1 Arrange the eggplant slices on a cutting board and sprinkle generously with salt. Let sit for about 20 minutes or until droplets of moisture appear on the surface of the eggplant. Rinse it off well, then pat dry the eggplant.

2 Heat 1 tablespoon of the oil in a heavy nonstick skillet over medium heat. Add as much of the eggplant that will fit in a single layer and not crowd each other. Brown the eggplant slices, moving them around so that they brown and cook through but do not burn. Turn and cook on the second side until that side too is lightly browned and the eggplant is tender when pierced with a fork. When eggplant is cooked, remove to a plate or pan, and continue adding eggplant until they are all cooked. Set aside for a few minutes.

3 Open up the rolls and pull a little of the fluffy insides out, then sprinkle each cut side with chopped garlic. On 1 side of each roll, place a slice or 2 of eggplant, then top with a leaf or 2 of basil, some ricotta cheese, a sprinkle of Parmesan, and a layer of mozzarella. Finish with sliced tomatoes; close up and press gently to seal together.

4 Heat the same skillet over medium-high heat or use a panini press, and lightly brush the sandwiches with a bit of olive oil on the outsides. Brown or grill the sandwiches, pressing as they brown and crisp. When the first side is browned through, turn over and brown the second side until the cheese is melted. Serve right away.

Grilled Eggplant and Chaumes,

with Marinated Peppers and Red Chili Aioli

RED CHILI AIOLI

2–3 cloves garlic, minced

4–6 tablespoons mayonnaise

Juice of ½ lemon or lime (about 1 tablespoon or to taste)

2–3 teaspoons chili powder

1 teaspoon paprika

½ teaspoon ground cumin

Large pinch dried oregano leaves, crushed

2 tablespoons extra-virgin olive oil

Several shakes smoky chile sauce such as Chipotle Tabasco, or Buffala

2 tablespoons coarsely chopped fresh cilantro

1 eggplant, cut crosswise into ¼- to ½-inch-thick slices

Olive oil

4 soft white or sourdough rolls, or 8 slices of country-style white or sourdough bread

¾ cup marinated roasted red and/or yellow peppers, preferably in brine (purchased, or homemade, page 104)

About 12 ounces semi-soft but flavorful cheese such as Chaumes, Bel Paese, Port-Salut, or Jack, cut into fat slices to fit onto the bread

Slices of crisp-edged browned eggplant are so delicious tucked into grilled cheese sandwiches that I tend to make a bit extra, just for next-day sandwich lunches such as this delicious goodie of melted mild cheese, marinated peppers, and creamy oozy spicy red chili aioli.

You can marinate your own red and yellow peppers (see page 104) or buy them in a jar, in brine. And I do think you'll find no end of uses for the red chili aioli, starting with the most obvious: a big fat burger and crisp French fries. Steamed crab and lobster, golden fish cakes, grilled chicken breasts, hard-cooked egg salad with boiled potatoes and watercress—all are delicious with the red chili aioli, too. I might think about a spicy swipe in other grilled cheese sandwiches too, perhaps something southern Italian involving salami, ham, provolone, mozzarella, and maybe even sliced grilled artichoke.

1 To make the Red Chili Aioli: In a small bowl, combine the garlic with the mayonnaise, lemon juice, chili powder, paprika, cumin, and oregano; stir well to combine. With your spoon or a whisk, beat in the olive oil, adding the oil a few teaspoons at a time and beating it until incorporated into the mixture before adding the rest. When smooth, shake in smoked chile sauce to taste, and finally stir in the cilantro. Cover and chill until ready to use. Makes about ⅓ cup.

2 To prepare the eggplant, lightly brush the eggplant slices with olive oil and heat a heavy nonstick skillet over medium-high heat. Pan brown the eggplant slices on each side until they are lightly browned and tender when pierced with a fork. Set aside.

3 To make the sandwiches: Lay out the open soft rolls and slather the red chili aioli generously on the insides. Layer eggplant slices on one side of the rolls, then the peppers, then a layer of the cheese. Close up and press together well. Lightly brush the outside of each sandwich with olive oil.

4 Heat the skillet again over medium-high heat, then add the sandwiches and reduce the heat to medium-low. Weight down the sandwiches (see Tip, page 22), and cook for a few minutes. When the bottom bread is golden and slightly browned in places, turn over and cook the other side, similarly weighted.

5 When that side too is golden and crisp, the cheese should be melted and gooey; it may be oozing out a bit and crisping as it does. (Don't discard these delicious crispy bits, just plop them onto each plate along with the sandwich.)

6 Remove the sandwiches to plates; cut into halves and serve.

Smoky Bacon and Cheddar

with Chipotle Relish

CHIPOTLE RELISH

½ onion, thinly sliced lengthwise

6 tablespoons ketchup

¼ cup mild vinegar such as white wine

3 tablespoons sugar

6 large cloves garlic, sliced

Generous pinch of ground cumin

Generous pinch of dried oregano leaves, crushed between the hands

Small pinch of cinnamon

Small pinch of ground cloves or allspice

Black pepper

Several big shakes of Worcestershire sauce

About 4 tablespoons chipotle sauce such as Tabasco or Buffala

SANDWICHES

8 pieces smoky bacon, preferably meaty lean bacon such as Canadian

8 large slices rustic country bread such as sourdough, sliced medium-thick

About 1 tablespoon brown mustard

8 ounces sharp Cheddar, thinly sliced

Olive oil for brushing bread

1–2 tablespoons chopped fresh cilantro

Smoky chipotle relish, a smear of tangy mustard, meaty smoky bacon, and strong pungent Cheddar—there's nothing subtle about this big-flavored sandwich. Try the chipotle relish on a hamburger, too! A glass of *cerveza* with a wedge of lime on the side comes close to perfection.

1 To make the Chipotle Relish (this can be done up to 2 days ahead of time and kept covered in the refrigerator): In a small heavy saucepan, combine the onions, ketchup, vinegar, sugar, and 3 tablespoons water. Bring to a boil, then simmer a few minutes, until the onions begin to soften and the liquid thickens.

2 Remove from the heat and add the garlic, cumin, oregano, cinnamon, cloves, black pepper, Worcestershire sauce, and as much chipotle sauce as you dare (I taste as I go). Makes ½ to ¾ cup.

3 To make the sandwiches: Brown the bacon in a heavy nonstick pan until it is cooked but not crisp—you will be finishing them under the broiler. Remove bacon from the pan and place on a piece of paper towel to drain.

4 Spread the mustard onto 1 side of 4 pieces of the bread. Top with the cheese, bacon, a smear of the Chipotle Relish, and the second pieces of bread. Press together well to seal the filling in.

5 Brush the outside of each sandwich with olive oil. Heat a heavy nonstick skillet or a sandwich press over medium-high heat. Lower heat to medium-low and brown the sandwiches, turning once or twice, pressing on the sandwiches gently with your spatula every so often if using a skillet, until the bread is crisp and golden and the cheese has melted.

6 Eat right away, with dabs of extra Chipotle Relish to taste, and a sprinkling of cilantro as garnish.

A layer of creamy wild mushroom sauce and a layer of cheese melt together into a rich, cheesy, mushroomy mixture. If desired, the sandwiches can be made open-faced: smear the wild mushrooms onto bread or prebaked pizza dough, top with the cheese, and broil. I like to use a Tuscan mild and youngish pecorino cheese for this sandwich. A medium Asiago or Mezzo Secco Jack are all good, as well, as would be fontina, whether domestic, Danish, or Italian. Serve with a crisp little salad of mixed greens such as the Spring Mix with Herbs (page 103).

1–1½ ounces dry porcini or cèpes, or mixed mushrooms including about half porcini or cèpes, broken in smallish pieces

About ½ cup heavy cream

Salt

A few grains of cayenne pepper

A few drops of fresh lemon juice

½ teaspoon cornstarch, mixed with 1 teaspoon water

8 slices pain au levain or other French bread

About 1 tablespoon soft butter for spreading on bread

2 cloves garlic, finely chopped

8–10 ounces sliced pecorino, fontina, or Mezzo Secco cheese

4 tablespoons freshly grated Parmesan cheese

About ¼ cup finely chopped fresh chives

1 In a heavy saucepan, combine the mushrooms and 2 cups of water. Bring to a boil, then reduce the heat and simmer until the liquid is nearly evaporated and the mushrooms are softened, 10 to 15 minutes. Stir in the cream and return to the heat for a few minutes, then season with salt, just a grain or two of cayenne, and just a drop or two of lemon juice. Stir in the cornstarch mixture and warm over medium-low heat until it thickens. It should thicken as soon as the edges begin to bubble. Because cream can vary in thickness, there is no way of knowing exactly how much cornstarch you will need. If the mixture is still liquidy after heating instead of very thick, add a little more cornstarch thinned down with a bit of the mushroom sauce or water. Once thick enough, leave mixture at room temperature to cool. It will thicken further as it cools. You want a thick spreadable consistency.

2 Lay out all of the bread and brush 1 side of each slice very lightly with the butter. Turn them all over, then on 4 of them, sprinkle the garlic. Top with the slices of pecorino, some of the chunks of mushrooms from the sauce, and a sprinkling of Parmesan. On the other 4 pieces of bread (unbuttered side), spread the mushroom sauce thickly. Close the sandwiches up tightly. The buttered sides will be on the outside.

3 Heat a heavy nonstick skillet over medium-low heat. Add the sandwiches, 1 or 2 at a time, depending on the size of the pan, and weight them with a heavy frying pan (see Tips, page 22).

4 Cook until the bread is golden and lightly browned in places, delightfully crisp, and the cheese is starting to ooze. Turn over and repeat until the second side is as golden and crisp as the first, adding the chopped garlic to the pan for the final minute or so of cooking. The cheese should be runny by now, with a few bits oozing out and lightly crisping at the edge of the crust.

5 Place on a plate, cut into halves or quarters, and sprinkle the plate with chives. Eat right away. There is nothing as sodden as a cold grilled cheese sandwich.

Wild Mushrooms and Melted Cheese on
Pain au Levain

4–6 marinated artichoke hearts, sliced

4 thick slices country bread, either sweet or sourdough

12 ounces provolone, firmish mozzarella, manouri, or other mild and meltable cheese, shredded

2 tablespoons extra-virgin olive oil

4 cloves garlic, very thinly sliced or minced

About 2 tablespoons red wine vinegar

1 tablespoon capers in brine, drained

1 teaspoon crumbled dried oregano

Several grindings black pepper

1–2 teaspoons chopped fresh flat-leaf parsley

Browned and melty, tangy with a splash of vinegar, a layer of marinated artichoke hearts, and the aroma of garlic, capers, and oregano, this grilled cheese is inspired by one I ate in Sicily. Sweet and Sour Roasted Peppers (page 104) on the side, definitely!

1 Preheat the broiler.

2 Arrange the artichokes on the bread and place on a baking sheet, then top with the cheese.

3 In a heavy nonstick skillet, heat the olive oil over medium-high heat, then add the garlic and lightly brown. Add the red wine vinegar, capers, oregano, and black pepper, and cook a minute or two, or until the liquid reduces to about 2 teaspoons. Stir in the parsley. Spoon over the cheese-topped bread.

4 Broil until the cheese melts, bubbles, and turns golden in spots. Eat right away.

Sicilian
Sizzled Cheese
with Capers and Artichokes

Big Fat Griddled Scaloppine

and Pesto Zucchini "Hero"

Two 4 to 5-ounce boneless skinless chicken breasts or cutlets of pork, turkey, or veal

Salt

Black pepper

2 tablespoons extra-virgin olive oil, divided

3 cloves garlic, chopped, divided

2 zucchini, very thinly sliced and patted dry

2 tablespoons basil pesto, or to taste

2 tablespoons grated Parmesan, grana, or locatelli Romano cheese

4 soft sourdough rolls, or four 6-inch pieces of focaccia, halved

8–10 ounces mozzarella, domestic or Danish fontina, or Jack cheese, sliced

Mamma-Mia! This is a knife-and-fork, big, sloppy, utterly satisfying sandwich. I like adding vegetables such as zucchini to a grilled cheese sandwich sometimes—it takes the dish from simple snack to proper meal, adding a rich and yet lighter quality to the dish.

1 Pound the meat with a meat mallet; if it is thick, slice the chicken into very thin pieces. Sprinkle with salt and pepper. Heat a heavy nonstick skillet over medium-high heat, then add 1 tablespoon of the oil, the meat, and finally about half of the garlic. Brown the meat quickly on 1 side, then the other, then remove from the pan, and pour any bits of juice and garlic over the meat.

2 Return the pan to medium-high heat, and add another teaspoon or so of the oil. Sauté the zucchini until it is just tender. Remove to a bowl; season with salt and pepper. When it is cool, stir in the remaining garlic, the pesto, and the Parmesan cheese. Leave mixture to cool in a bowl; rinse and dry the pan.

3 With your fingers, tear out a little bit of the fluffy insides of each roll to make way for the filling. Heat the pan again over medium-high and lightly toast the cut sides of each roll. You will have to press them a bit; they may tear a little, but that is okay. They'll go back together again as they are browned and pressed with their filling in place.

4 Into half of each roll, stuff several tablespoons of the zucchini-pesto mixture, then top with a layer of the meat and the mozzarella. Close up and press together tightly to seal well.

5 Brush the remaining oil on the outsides of the sandwiches. Heat the pan again over medium-high heat. Weight sandwiches (see Tip, page 22) to help press them down and keep them together. Reduce the heat to medium-low and cook until the first side is crisp and golden and the cheese begins to melt. Turn over and repeat. Serve when the sandwiches are crisply golden and the cheese is melting seductively.

Quesadilla of Goat Cheese and Cilantro-Mint Ginger Chutney, PAGE 86

Quesadillas, Piadine, and Pita Sandwiches

The sandwiches in this chapter all have one thing in common: They are flat! And flatbreads—filled with spunky chutneys or spicy salsas, grilled vegetables or bright condiments along with melted cheese—make melty cheese parcels with a completely different quality than grilled cheese sandwiches on regular yeast-risen bread. Flatbreads are thinner and crisper, all about the gooey savory filling rather than the heft of bread. Indeed, they are sandwiches, yet not exactly sandwiches.

Pita, piadine, tortillas, and naan are all flat, and all delicious filled with or blanketed beneath melty cheese. Try using flatbreads interchangeably, too; what can go onto a pizza is delicious on top of a flour tortilla, while tortillas make a great substitute for the Italian flatbreads called piadine. Pita can take the place of tortillas and Middle Eastern flatbreads, and the Indian naan are delicious with all zesty flavors regardless of which continent they hail from.

Quesadilla of Goat Cheese and Cilantro-Mint Ginger Chutney

3 cloves garlic, chopped

About 1-inch piece fresh ginger, coarsely chopped (about 2 teaspoons)

3–4 tablespoons coarsely chopped fresh mint leaves

3–4 tablespoons coarsely chopped fresh cilantro

3 tablespoons plain yogurt

½ teaspoon sugar, or to taste

Large pinch of salt

Several good shakes of Tabasco or other hot sauce, or ½ fresh chile, chopped

8 flour tortillas

12 ounces fresh goat cheese with a rind such as Lezay or Montrachet, sliced ½ to ¾ inch thick

Olive oil for brushing tortillas

Fresh cilantro-mint chutney is aromatic and brightly flavored; layer with goat cheese and fill a couple of flour tortillas, then flash in your pan! Serve as a nibble, especially as an appetizer before a curry-spiced dinner. Make a fresh Italian Tomato Salad (page 103) to go with it.

1 In a food processor or blender purée the garlic with the ginger, then add the mint, cilantro, yogurt, sugar, salt, and hot sauce. Whirl until it forms a green, slightly chunky paste.

2 Lay out 4 tortillas, and spread them first with the cilantro-mint mixture, then a layer of the goat cheese, and top with the other tortillas.

3 Lightly brush the outside of each sandwich with olive oil and cook, one at a time, in a heavy nonstick skillet over medium heat. Brown several minutes, until lightly golden in spots, pressing down on them a bit with the spatula as they cook. Flip over carefully using the spatula; when the second side is speckled with brown and gold, the cheese should be melted. Remove from the pan and cut into wedges. Serve immediately.

Fresh Mozzarella, Tomato, Thai Basil, and Gorgonzola Piadine

4 piadine or medium (12-inch) flour tortillas

3–4 tablespoons tomato paste

1 large ripe tomato, thinly sliced

1–2 cloves garlic, chopped

4–6 ounces fresh mozzarella cheese, sliced

About 12 leaves Thai or Vietnamese basil (or ordinary basil)

About 3 ounces Gorgonzola cheese, sliced or crumbled

2–3 tablespoons freshly grated Parmesan or other grating cheese such as Asiago or grana

Extra-virgin olive oil for drizzling

This pizza-like piadina is enticing indeed. Thai or Vietnamese basil gives the sandwich a slightly unusual twist; it tastes like the essence of the Mediterranean, and yet, the exotic aroma of Asia combines with the flavors of tomato and Gorgonzola, creating a completely different basil experience. Serve a red and white Whole Leaf Endive Salad (page 103) on the side.

1 Preheat the broiler.

2 Lay the piadine out on 1 or 2 baking sheets and spread them with a bit of the tomato paste, then layer with a small amount of the tomato, and sprinkle with the garlic. Top with the mozzarella, basil, and Gorgonzola, sprinkle with the Parmesan, then drizzle with olive oil.

3 Broil, working in batches if necessary, until the cheese melts and the sandwiches are sizzling hot. Serve right away.

Picadillo and Jack
Quesadillas on Pumpkin Tortillas

- 2 large mild green chiles such as Anaheim or poblano, or 2 green bell peppers
- 1 onion, chopped
- 2 cloves garlic, chopped
- 1 tablespoon extra-virgin olive oil
- 1 pound lean ground beef
- 1/8–1/4 teaspoon ground cinnamon, or to taste
- 1/4 teaspoon ground cumin
- Pinch of ground cloves or allspice
- 1/3 cup dry sherry, or dry red wine
- 1/4 cup raisins
- 2 tablespoons tomato paste
- 2 tablespoons sugar
- A few shakes of red wine or sherry vinegar
- Salt
- Black pepper
- A few shakes of cayenne, or Tabasco if using bell peppers instead of chiles
- 1/4 cup coarsely chopped almonds
- 2–3 tablespoons coarsely chopped fresh cilantro, plus extra for garnishing
- 8 pumpkin tortillas
- 6–8 ounces mild cheese such as Jack, manchego, or Mezzo Secco
- Olive oil for brushing tortillas
- About 2 tablespoons sour cream for garnishing

Party fare extraordinaire! Make them big, make them little and dainty, serve them with wine, or iced sherry, or with chilled lager! The combination of sweet, spicy, meaty, tangy, and nutty is delicious, with its layer of cheese and mild green chile, all sandwiched between two slightly sweet and earthy pumpkin tortillas.

Pumpkin tortillas are the brainchild of Rancho Santa Fe products. I discovered them at the Davis Farmer's Market in California one Saturday, and have been watching with delight as they appear in more and more supermarket and natural foods shops throughout the Bay Area. They freeze excellently, so when you find them, buy a stack and stash them in your freezer. If you can't find pumpkin tortillas, use regular flour tortillas and add a layer of thinly sliced, sautéed, peeled pumpkin. Ditto for the picadillo: make a double batch and pack it up into the deep freeze.

1 Roast the chiles or peppers over an open flame until they are charred lightly and evenly all over. Place in a plastic bag or bowl, and cover. Set aside for at least 30 minutes, as the steam helps separate the skins from the flesh.

2 Prepare the picadillo: Sauté the onion and garlic in the olive oil over medium heat until softened, then add the beef and cook together, stirring and breaking up the meat as you cook. When the meat is browned in spots, sprinkle with the cinnamon, cumin, and cloves and continue cooking and stirring.

3 Add the sherry, raisins, tomato paste, sugar, and vinegar. Cook together for about 15 minutes, stirring every so often; if it seems dry, add a little water or more sherry. Season with salt, pepper, and cayenne, and adjust the sugar and vinegar to taste. Add the almonds and cilantro and set aside.

4 Remove the skin, stems, and seeds from the peppers, then cut the peppers into strips.

5 Lay out 4 of the tortillas and spread with the picadillo. Add the roasted pepper strips, then a layer of the cheese, and top each with a second tortilla. Press down firmly to hold them together.

6 Heat a heavy nonstick skillet over medium-high heat. Brush the outsides of the quesadillas lightly with olive oil and add them to the pan, working in batches. Lower the heat to medium-low, brown on one side, then carefully turn over using the spatula with guidance from your hand if needed. Cook on the second side until golden in spots and the cheese is melted.

7 Serve immediately, cut into wedges, garnished with a dollop of sour cream and cilantro.

Peppers, Pepperoni, Provolone, and Pecorino Pita!

4 pitas
½ cup roasted, peeled, and sliced red and/or yellow peppers
2 cloves garlic, chopped
4 ounces pepperoni, thinly sliced
4 ounces provolone cheese, diced
2 tablespoons freshly grated pecorino cheese
4 Italian or Greek pickled peppers such as pepperoncini, thinly sliced
Olive oil for brushing pita

Forgive the overdose of alliteration, I couldn't help myself. I was lucky to stop where I did, there were so many more "p" words just calling out to me. Meanwhile, just make this sandwich: layers of spicy cured meat such as pepperoni, a nice assemblage of pickled and roasted peppers, and a whiff of garlic, all stuffed into a pita and pressed into hot melty madness. Yum.

1 Slit 1 side of each pita and open them to form pockets.

2 Layer the peppers, garlic, pepperoni, provolone, pecorino, and peppers into each pita and press to close. Brush the outsides lightly with olive oil.

3 Heat a heavy nonstick skillet over medium-high heat or use a sandwich maker or panini press.

Place the sandwiches into the pan. Reduce the heat to low and weight the sandwiches down (see Tip, page 22), pressing as you brown them. Cook only until the cheese melts; you don't want the cheeses to brown and crisp, simply to hold all the fillings together.

4 Serve right away.

Grilled Sheep Cheese Quesadillas with Fresh Tarragon and Ripe Tomatoes

8 big flour tortillas
1 tablespoon chopped fresh tarragon
2 large ripe tomatoes, thinly sliced
8–10 ounces slightly dry sheep cheese such as an aged Cheddar or Idiazábel, or a cow cheese such as an aged Gouda or a Swaledale, shredded
Olive oil, for brushing tortillas

This is a quirky combination that came about one day when I had these ingredients on hand and, in the way of these serendipitous concoctions, it worked deliciously: herbal tarragon, tangy tomato, and sharp funky cheese. The cheese I used was a homemade sheep cheese from Cyprus. Since you're unlikely to have the exact same cheese, choose any nice sharpish sheep or goat cheese, or choose a flavorful dryish cow cheese such as Vella Mezzo Secco, or dry Jack combined with a bit of Asiago.

1 Lay the tortillas out on a work surface, sprinkle with the tarragon, and layer with the tomatoes. Top with the cheese and cover each with a second tortilla.

2 Brush each sandwich with olive oil, and heat a heavy nonstick skillet or flat grill over medium heat. Working 1 at a time, cook the quesadilla on 1 side; when it is flecked lightly with golden brown and the cheese is melting, turn it over and cook the second side, pressing as it cooks to flatten it. It is ready when the cheese has melted and the tortillas are golden browned in spots. Repeat with the remaining quesadillas.

3 Serve immediately, cut into wedges.

Last Days of the Raj:
Grilled Cheddar,
Chutney, Sausage, and Cilantro

1–2 savory spicy herby sausages (about 9 ounces total), sliced diagonally into ½-inch slices

4 whole-wheat pitas, the pockets opened up

3–4 tablespoons sweet and spicy mango chutney such as Major Grey's, the big pieces of fruit diced, plus extra for dabbing on as desired

2 tablespoons chopped fresh cilantro

6–8 ounces mature Cheddar cheese, coarsely shredded

1 tablespoon olive oil for brushing bread

3 tablespoons shelled toasted sunflower seeds, preferably unsalted

The name refers to the cross-cultural Anglo-Indian flavors of this sandwich and the end of the British rule of India. From the many years that Britain ruled India, a whole cuisine combining Indian and English flavors evolved; dishes such as Mulligatawny soup fall into this category, as does this nifty little sandwich combination in which Anglo cheese meets Indian chutney and fresh coriander (cilantro), while British sausage meets a whiff of nippy spice. Moroccan Carrot Relish (page 103) is nice alongside.

Choose from the wide range of sausages available these days: curry-scented chicken or turkey ones will be particularly good, as will smoked varieties, even kielbasa. All stuffed into a whole-wheat pita and scattered with toasted sunflower seeds, it's a fetching little sandwich indeed.

1 Brown the sliced sausages in a skillet over medium heat. Set them aside to drain on paper towels.

2 Arrange the pitas on a work surface. Spread 1 half of the inside with the chutney, then add the sausage, cilantro, and finally the cheese. Press lightly to close, and brush the outsides with olive oil.

3 Heat a heavy nonstick skillet over medium-high heat or use a panini press. Add the stuffed pitas and press lightly; reduce heat to medium or even medium-low. Cook on 1 side until lightly golden in spots and the cheese is melting; turn over and lightly brown on the second side. When cheese is melted, remove from the pan.

4 Serve right away, sprinkled with sunflower seeds, and offer additional chutney on the side for dabbing.

Hot Prosciutto and Taleggio with Ripe Figs on Mesclun, **PAGE 92**

Grilled Cheese in Salad

Grilled cheese sandwiches, crisp, rich, and oozing melted cheese, are delicious paired with a tuft of greenery, a handful of lettuces, a scattering of herbs—in other words, a salad. It's a small hop from sitting next to a salad, to being a part of the salad itself! Here we have melted cheesy toasts, plopped deliciously into leafy little salads. The hot cheese, the crisp toast, the fresh leaves . . . mmmm . . . divine.

Hot Prosciutto and Taleggio

with Ripe Figs on Mesclun

- 8 very thin slices of sourdough bread or baguette
- 3 tablespoons extra-virgin olive oil, divided
- 3–4 ounces prosciutto, cut into 8 slices
- 8 ounces ripe Taleggio cheese, sliced into eight ¼-inch-thick pieces
- 4 big handfuls of salad spring mix (mesclun)
- 2 tablespoons chopped fresh chives
- 2 tablespoons chopped fresh chervil
- 1 tablespoon fresh lemon juice
  Salt
  Black pepper
- 6 ripe black figs, quartered
- 1–2 teaspoons balsamic vinegar

This sandwich was inspired by a dish prepared by visiting chefs at Parma's prosciutto festival, held every summer. The rolling hills of Parma, Italy, are home of the pig, the source of that region's delicious prosciutto: in fact, said my hosts, "Parma is all about the pig; in fact, the prosciutto is even more tasty because they grow up eating the whey left over from making Parma's other delicacy—Parmigiano cheese." It's all very ecologically balanced, and of course, delicious. Another ingredient in this salad, balsamic vinegar, is from Modena, just down the road from Parma.

1 Lightly brush the bread with a tiny amount of the olive oil and arrange on a baking sheet.

2 Preheat the oven to 400ºF. Place the bread on the highest rack and bake about 5 minutes, or until they are just beginning to crisp. Remove and let cool, about 10 minutes.

3 When cool, wrap the prosciutto slices around the Taleggio slices and set each one atop a piece of bread. Set aside a moment while you prepare the salad.

4 Mix the greens with about 1 tablespoon of olive oil, the chives, and the chervil, then toss with the lemon juice, salt, and pepper to taste. Arrange on 4 plates and garnish with the fig quarters.

5 Brush the tops of the prosciutto-wrapped parcels with the remaining olive oil, then place in a large ovenproof skillet and bake for 5 to 7 minutes, or until the cheese begins to ooze and the prosciutto crisps around the edges. Quickly remove the parcels and arrange on each salad, then shake the balsamic vinegar into the hot pan. Swirl so that it warms, then pour it over the salads and toasts. Serve right away.

8 slices sourdough bread

About 6 ounces bresaola, thinly sliced

6–8 ounces nutty, flavorful, melting cheese such as fontina, Jarlsberg, or Emmentaler

About 4 cups mixed baby arugula and mizuna, or other tender greens such as spring mix

2 ripe but firm pears, thinly sliced or julienned, tossed in a little lemon juice to keep them from browning

1 shallot, minced

1 tablespoon balsamic vinegar

2 tablespoons extra-virgin olive oil, plus more for brushing

Salt

Black pepper

Ultra-savory thin cured beef, *bresaola* is much like a beef version of prosciutto: salty, meaty, and full of vivacious flavor. Here, it is melted with fontina between the covers of sourdough, then plopped onto a plate of arugula, mizuna, and pears. The balance of salty, nutty, crisp, hot, and melty, alongside fresh leafy green and juicy sweet, is divine.

1 Arrange 4 pieces of the bread on a work surface and on 1 side lay the bresaola, then top with the cheese, and finish by topping with the other slices of sourdough. Press together lightly but firmly to seal.

2 Meanwhile, mix the greens in a bowl with the sliced pears. Set aside.

3 In a small bowl, mix the shallot with the balsamic vinegar and 2 tablespoons of olive oil, then season with salt and pepper to taste. Set aside.

4 Brush the sandwiches with a small amount of the olive oil. Heat a sandwich press or heavy nonstick skillet over medium-high heat, then place the sandwiches in the pan. You'll probably need to do this in 2 batches. Weight the sandwiches (see Tip, page 22). Cook until the bread is crisp and golden, then turn over and repeat on the second side, until the cheese is melted.

5 Just before sandwiches are ready, toss the salad with the dressing. Distribute the salad among 4 plates. When the sandwiches are ready, remove from the pan, cut into quarters, and place 4 on each plate of salad.

6 Serve right away.

Grilled Bresaola and Fontina

with Arugula, Mizuna, and Fresh Pears

Open-Faced
Chèvre Sandwiches
in Salad with Walnut Vinaigrette

Chèvre chaud, or hot goat cheese—topped toasts on salad—is a classic of the Paris cafés and bistros. It is varied in small ways, endlessly—for instance the type of chèvre, whether fresh and softly tangy, or pungent and slightly aged, or funky and firm. Then there are the greens and the added salad ingredients: bits of hot bacon, slices of raw onion, wedges of tomato, sliced potato, and so forth. At its heart, though, chèvre chaud is simply a green salad topped with a couple of hot open-faced grilled goat cheese sandwiches. It's something you can always count on for delicious sustenance in the streets of Paris or in your own kitchen.

About ½ baguette, cut into 12 diagonal slices about ½-inch thick

2 tablespoons extra-virgin olive oil, or as needed

3 ounces goat cheese with a rind, such as Lezay, sliced ¼- to ½-inch thick

Generous pinch of dried or fresh thyme leaves

Black pepper

1 tablespoon red wine vinegar, divided

About 6 cups mixed greens, such as spring mix, including a bit of young frisée and arugula

2 tablespoons chopped fresh parsley, chives, chervil, or a combination

1 tablespoon walnut oil

¼ cup walnut pieces

1 Preheat the broiler.

2 Brush the baguette slices with a little of the olive oil, then set them on a baking sheet and broil for about 5 minutes, or until golden on 1 side only. Remove from the broiler.

3 Turn the toasted bread over and on the untoasted sides, place a slice or 2 of the goat cheese. The amount you use per sandwich will depend on how big your baguette slices are. Drizzle the tops with a tiny bit of olive oil, sprinkle on the thyme and black pepper, then shake a few drops of the vinegar over the cheeses.

4 Meanwhile, toss the salad with the chopped herbs and dress with the walnut oil and the remaining olive oil and vinegar, and sprinkle with the walnut pieces. Arrange on 4 big plates or in shallow soup bowls.

5 Place the goat cheese–topped toasts under the broiler and broil for about 5 minutes, or until the cheese is softened and the top just begins to bubble in places, the color of the cheese tinged golden brown.

6 Immediately place 3 hot goat cheese sandwiches on top of the dressed salad on each plate, and serve right away.

VARIATION *Goat Cheese Toasts Sprinkled with Diced Fresh Pear and Dried Cranberry*

To the above mixture of greens, add 1 diced fresh pear, some dried cranberries, and a handful of peppery sprouts such as broccoli sprouts, cress, or other pungent tiny greens.

Sizzled Halloumi
Sandwiches with Lime
on a Summer-Day Salad

Halloumi is a deliciously rubbery cheese that does not melt when heated; as a result it is delicious barbecued, fried, or broiled as it will never melt and fall apart! Fried halloumi is one of the national dishes of Cyprus, and it is salty, savory, and sublime, hot from the pan. While traditionally it is served with a squeeze of lemon, I recently tried it with lime and it was wonderful.

Here we've tossed it into a salad to make that wonderful combination of hot and salty, cool and tender, and refreshing that warm salads are all about. If you are unable to find halloumi, by the way, use the Hispanic cheese called panela. It is not as salty as halloumi, but it sizzles as deliciously. In fact, you might find you prefer it!

TIP When heating rubbery cheeses such as this, you must eat the cheese hot, hot, hot; warm, sizzling, and chewy is good, cold and hard chewy is not.

1 head butter or Boston Bibb lettuce, trimmed and separated into leaves

1 mild white onion, peeled and thinly sliced crosswise

4 tablespoons extra-virgin olive oil, divided

1 teaspoon white wine vinegar

3 large ripe tomatoes, cut into wedges

Salt

Black pepper

½ baguette, cut into 12 diagonal slices about ½-inch thick

12 ounces halloumi, sliced about ½ inch thick

2 limes, cut into wedges (or about 2 tablespoons fresh lime juice)

A pinch dried oregano

1 Preheat the broiler.

2 In a big bowl, toss together the lettuce and onion, then dress with about 2 tablespoons of the olive oil and the vinegar. Divide among 4 plates, then garnish each with tomato wedges; sprinkle salads with salt and pepper and set aside.

3 Brush the baguette slices with some of the olive oil, place on a baking sheet, and broil lightly on both sides. Set aside.

4 Arrange the halloumi on a baking sheet and brush with some olive oil. Broil on 1 side until browned in spots, then remove. Turn over each slice of cheese and place on top of a toast, then brush with olive oil again and return to the broiler. Broil until hot and lightly browned in spots.

5 Place 3 hot halloumi-topped toasts on each salad, squeeze lime juice over the halloumi, and let a little bit drizzle onto the salads. Sprinkle with oregano and serve.

Truffled Hot
St. Marcellin Toast
and Arugula Salad

4 fairly thick slices pain au levain, each slice quartered

About 2 teaspoons truffle oil, or to taste (the flavors of different truffle oils tend to vary widely)

2 ripe St. Marcellin cheeses (about 2½ ounces each)

A pinch of salt

About 8 ounces young arugula leaves (about 4 cups loosely packed)

2 tablespoons extra-virgin olive oil

A few shakes of sherry vinegar

This salad whipped itself up in my kitchen one afternoon. I'd had St. Marcellin on my mind for awhile, so a few days previously I had bought one "just in case." It was hanging out in my refrigerator . . . awaiting inspiration. The truffle oil was the result of a recent visit to France, and as I always have pain au levain stashed away in my freezer for moments like this, all I needed was the deliciously fresh arugula found at my local market.

1 Preheat the oven to 400ºF.

2 Arrange the pieces of pain au levain on a baking sheet and lightly toast in the oven on both sides. Remove from the oven and sprinkle each with a bit of the truffle oil, then place about 1 tablespoon of the St. Marcellin cheese atop each toast. (Each person will end up with about ½ of a cheese.) Sprinkle the cheese lightly with a pinch of salt. Return to the oven for a few moments.

3 Meanwhile, arrange the arugula on 4 plates. Shake over each plate a bit of olive oil, a bit of truffle oil, and a few drops here and there of sherry vinegar. Don't toss, simply let the droplets lie on the plates.

4 Remove the cheese toasts from the oven after only 30 to 45 seconds. You do not want the cheese to melt completely or sizzle and go oily; you want it to simply become a bit warm and creamy.

5 Place 4 hot toasts onto each salad plate and serve immediately.

French Toast Stuffed with Strawberries and Cream Cheese, PAGE 100

Sweeties

Grilled cheese sandwiches don't have to be savory, they can be sweet, too! Whether stuffed with goat cheese and strawberry jam then dipped in egg à la French toast, or inspired by the Mexican bread pudding *capirotada*, stuffed with melted Jack and dripping in caramel . . . sweet grilled cheese is quite fetching. Enjoy for brunch, for tea, or for a midnight snack; it's pretty much anytime-you-want-it fare!

French Toast

Stuffed with Strawberries and Cream Cheese

8 medium-thick slices soft, sweet white bread, such as challah or brioche

8–12 tablespoons (about 8 ounces) cream cheese (low fat is fine)

About ½ cup strawberry preserves

1 cup (about 10 ounces) sliced strawberries

2 large eggs, lightly beaten

1 egg yolk

About ½ cup milk (low fat is fine)

A dash vanilla extract

Sugar

2–4 tablespoons unsalted butter

½ teaspoon fresh lemon juice

½ cup sour cream

Several sprigs fresh mint, thinly sliced

The combination of cream cheese and strawberries is one of life's inspired pairings: sweet, tangy, and fruity, balanced with rich and creamy. Dip the sandwiches into egg-and-milk, like French toast, and you have a perfect Sunday-morning brunch.

1 Spread 4 slices of the bread thickly with the cream cheese, tapering a bit towards the sides so that the cream cheese doesn't seep out in the cooking, then spread the other 4 slices of bread with the preserves. Scatter a light layer of strawberries over the top of the cream cheese (reserve the rest of the strawberries for the topping). Top each piece of cheese-spread bread with a preserve-spread piece of bread. Press gently but firmly to seal.

2 In a shallow bowl, combine the eggs, egg yolk, milk, vanilla extract, and about 1 tablespoon of sugar.

3 Heat a heavy nonstick skillet over medium-high heat. Add the butter. Dip each sandwich, 1 at a time, into the bowl with the milk and egg. Let it soak in a moment or 2, then turn over and repeat.

4 Place the sandwiches into the hot pan with the melted butter and let them cook to a golden brown. Turn over and lightly brown the second sides.

5 Meanwhile, combine the remaining strawberries with sugar to taste and the lemon juice.

6 Serve each sandwich as soon as it's done, garnished with a spoonful or 2 of the strawberries and a dollop of the sour cream. Sprinkle them with some of the mint as well.

The classic Mexican-American bread pudding *(capirotada)* with spices, fruit, and nuts, as well as creamy cheese, is sort of a baked grilled cheese sandwich pudding. Here we've reversed things and returned pudding to sandwich. Slightly stale bread is best, by the way.

¾ cup packed light brown sugar

¼ cup sugar, divided

5–6 cloves

⅛ teaspoon ground cinnamon, plus extra for shaking on top

1 large tangy apple such as Granny Smith, unpeeled and thinly sliced

¼ cup raisins

½ teaspoon vanilla extract

8 thick (¾- to 1-inch) slices French bread, preferably stale

6–8 ounces mild meltable cheese such as Jack, or a very mild white Cheddar, sliced

½ cup slivered blanched almonds or pine nuts

About 3 tablespoons butter

1 tablespoon olive oil

1 In a heavy-bottomed saucepan, combine the brown sugar with 2 tablespoons of the sugar, the cloves, and the cinnamon. Add 2 cups of water and stir to mix well.

2 Place over a medium-high heat and bring to a boil, then reduce the heat to medium-low, until the liquid forms a light bubbling simmer. Cook for 15 minutes, or until it forms a thinnish syrup. Add the apple slices and raisins, then cook a further 5 minutes. Remove from the heat and add the vanilla.

3 Arrange the slices of bread on a work surface. Spoon hot syrup over each piece of bread, several tablespoons per piece. Carefully turn each piece over and spoon hot syrup over the second sides. Leave for about 30 minutes.

4 Spoon a bit more syrup onto the bread, again about one tablespoon or so per slice of bread. The bread will become quite soft and risk falling apart as it absorbs the sweet syrup, so take care when handling it. Leave a further 15 minutes or so.

5 Place one slice of cheese on top of 4 slices of the soaked bread. Top each with about ¼ of the

apples, raisins, and a sprinkling of almonds (reserve some for the end). Top with the remaining slices of bread to form 4 sandwiches. Press together.

6 Heat a heavy nonstick skillet over medium-high heat, then add about 1 tablespoon each of butter and olive oil. When butter foams and browns, add the sandwiches. Reduce the heat to medium and cook, pressing gently with the spatula. Adjust the heat as the sandwiches brown, lowering it as needed to keep the sugar in the syrup browning but not burning. Turn the sandwiches several times, adding more butter to the pan, taking care that the sandwiches do not fall apart as you turn them. Press every so often, until the outsides of the sandwiches are browned and crisp and the cheese has melted.

7 A minute or 2 before they reach this state, toss the remaining almonds into the pan and let them lightly toast and brown. Sprinkle the sandwiches and the almonds with the remaining 2 tablespoons sugar. It gives a nice sweet accent and crispness, and helps cover up any bits of the sandwich that look *too* brown (with hot sugar, this is easy to do).

8 Serve immediately, each sandwich sprinkled with the toasted almonds.

Mexican-Style Cheese-Filled
Bread Pudding
Sandwiches

Tomato Soup, **PAGE 104**

Accompaniments

All sorts of things go with a grilled cheese sandwiches; crisp little salads, very interesting mustards, spunky salsas and chutneys, roasted peppers, and bread-and-butter pickles . . . and of course, the classic accompaniment that any grilled cheese could ask for—tomato soup!

Nine Simple Salads
to Eat Alongside Grilled Cheese Sandwiches

PARIS CAFÉ SALAD Mâche (lamb's lettuce) or watercress, roasted beets, and chopped shallots; dress with extra-virgin olive oil or a mixture of half olive oil and half walnut oil, and a bit of wine vinegar.

WHOLE ENDIVE LEAF SALAD Whole fronds of red or white endive or Treviso; dress with lemon juice, a sprinkling of salt, a splash of extra-virgin olive oil, and wine vinegar. Eat with your fingers.

SPRING MIX WITH HERBS Mesclun, mixed with chopped herbs (chervil, tarragon, flat-leaf parsley, chives). Dress with extra-virgin olive oil, a smidge of both balsamic and sherry vinegars, a clove of chopped garlic, and a little mustard. Serve with Taleggio and Fontina with the Scent of White Truffle (page 26).

ARUGULA SALAD Young arugula leaves, dressed with extra-virgin olive oil and a dash of balsamic vinegar, plus a sprinkle of salt and pepper. This has a simple big flavor, delicious with almost any grilled cheese. Try it with the Harry's Bar Special (page 42) for a light meal.

MEDITERRANEAN GREEN BEAN AND BLACK OLIVE SALAD Juicy al dente green beans, studded with salty black olives, tossed with a little chopped onion and dressed with extra-virgin olive oil and sherry vinegar. Serve with Garlic Grilled Cheese on Rye (page 30) or A Hot Muffaletta (page 60).

ITALIAN TOMATO SALAD Ripe, ripe tomatoes, topped with chopped fresh chives, mint, and basil, or simply sprinkled with crushed dried oregano. Garnish with a drop or two of balsamic vinegar and salt. Serve with Bruschetta from an Olive Grove in Puglia (page 45).

SUMMER REFRESHMENT ITSELF This "Caesarette" is a big bowl of Romaine leaves dressed with extra-virgin olive oil, lemon juice, chopped garlic, a dash of brown mustard, a dab of mayo to emulsify the mixture and get it to cling to the leaves, and a generous grating of Parmesan, pecorino, or dry Jack cheese. Serve with the "Club Class" Sandwich (page 55).

YELLOW PEPPERS AND BASIL Crosswise slices of yellow bell peppers topped with a flurry of julienned basil leaves. You don't even have to dress it! It's fresh, sweet, juicy, and fragrant, perfect to eat with your fingers alongside any grilled cheese, especially one with a spunky blue cheese inside, such as the Casse Croûte (page 46).

MOROCCAN CARROT RELISH Cook 2 carrots whole by either steaming or boiling until they are half cooked, that is, not quite tender. Dice them, toss with a chopped garlic clove or 2, a sprinkle of both ground cumin and cinnamon, a teaspoon or so of extra-virgin olive oil, a dash of wine vinegar, salt, and sugar to taste. Sprinkle or toss with a tablespoon of chopped fresh cilantro and chill until ready to enjoy. Serve with Grilled Jack on Rye with Green Olive Mustard (page 27) or Goat Cheese Toasts with Desert Spices (page 49).

Index

Table of Equivalents

The exact equivalents in the following tables have been rounded for convenience.

LIQUID/DRY MEASURES

U.S.	METRIC
¼ teaspoon	1.25 milliliters
½ teaspoon	2.5 milliliters
1 teaspoon	5 milliliters
1 tablespoon (3 teaspoons)	15 milliliters
1 fluid ounce (2 tablespoons)	30 milliliters
¼ cup	60 milliliters
⅓ cup	80 milliliters
½ cup	120 milliliters
1 cup	240 milliliters
1 pint (2 cups)	480 milliliters
1 quart (4 cups, 32 ounces)	960 milliliters
1 gallon (4 quarts)	3.84 liters
1 ounce (by weight)	28 grams
1 pound	454 grams
2.2 pounds	1 kilogram

OVEN TEMPERATURE

°F	°C	GAS
250	120	½
275	140	1
300	150	2
325	160	3
350	180	4
375	190	5
400	200	6
425	220	7
450	230	8
475	240	9
500	260	10

LENGTH

U.S.	METRIC
⅛ inch	3 millimeters
¼ inch	6 millimeters
½ inch	12 millimeters
1 inch	2.5 centimeters